Morton Rhue

Ghetto Kidz

Morton Rue wurde 1950 in New York geboren. Der mehrfach preisgekrönte Autor einer Vielzahl von Romanen für Jugendliche ist in Deutschland vor allem durch »Die Welle« bekannt geworden. Nach seinem Literaturstudium verdiente er seinen Lebensunterhalt teilweise als Straßenmusiker in Europa, später arbeitete er vornehmlich als Journalist. Heute widmet er sich fast ausschließlich seiner schriftstellerischen Tätigkeit neben Lesungen und Workshops in Schulen.

Von Morton Rhue sind im Ravensburger Taschenbuch erschienen:

RTB 58008
Die Welle

RTB 58172
Ich knall euch ab

RTB 58212
Asphalt Tribe

RTB 58213
Asphalt Tribe
(englische Ausgabe)

RTB 58255
Boot Camp

RTB 58256
Boot Camp
(englische Ausgabe)

RTB 58355
Ghetto Kidz

Morton Rhue

Ghetto Kidz

Afterword by the author

Ravensburger Buchverlag

Als Ravensburger Taschenbuch
Band 58356
erschienen 2010

Die Erstausgabe erschien 2008
im Ravensburger Buchverlag

Published by arrangement with
Todd Strasser

Lektorat: Petra Deistler
Glossar: Christina Sarembe
Umschlaggestaltung: Dirk Lieb
unter Verwendung eines Fotos von
Pjotr Sikora, getty images

Printed in Germany

1 2 3 4 5 14 13 12 11 10

ISBN 978-3-473-58356-0

www.ravensburger.de

“We’ve been spending most of our lives living in a gangsta’s paradise.”

Coolio

TWELVE YEARS OLD

The divisions between black and white, and rich and poor, begin at birth and are reinforced every day of a child's life.

division: Unterschied **to reinforce:** bestätigen, verstärken

One

The shouting and screaming outside started at dinnertime. We were sitting on the living room couch eating macaroni and cheese and watching *Judge Joe Brown* on the TV. Between the hissing and banging of the heat pipes and the noise outside, it was one big racket.

"Kalon, turn up the sound," Gramma said. I put my tray on the couch, picked up the clicker and turned up the volume. It was just me and Gramma that night. My big sister Nia was out with her boyfriend Denzel.

Outside the yelling got louder and the police sirens started. Gramma flinched and put down her fork. "Noise around here is gonna make me lose my mind."

But the sounds made me curious and I glanced toward the thick green curtains that covered the window.

10 **Judge Joe Brown:** Gerichtsfernsehen 11 **to hiss:** zischen **to bang:** klopfen **heat pipes:** Heizungsrohre
12 **racket:** Heidenlärm 13 **Gramma:** ugs. für Grandmother
14 **clicker:** (ugs.) Fernbedienung 17 **to yell:** (herum-)schreien
18 **to flinch:** zusammenzucken

Ever since gangbangers cocktailed the apartment down the hall, Gramma kept the curtains closed all the time.

"Don't go near that window," Gramma warned. "They start shooting, you'll get shot."

In the curtains were two holes the size of bottle caps where bullets had come through before. There were bullet holes in the walls, too. Gramma had put a picture over one of them and our little Christmas tree decorated with tinsel and candy canes blocked the other. Gramma said we'd be safer living on a high floor, but the elevators were always broken and it was hard for her to climb the stairs after cleaning houses all day. In the projects, the older you got, the closer you had to live to the ground.

The sirens and shouting outside got louder. I gave Gramma a pleading look.

"No," she said firmly.

"But the police are here," I argued. "Won't be any shooting."

"I said no." But lately she always sounded weary and defeated, and I knew I could wear her down.

"Come on, *please*?" I said. Outside the sirens had

1 **gangbanger:** Bandenmitglied **to cocktail:** (ugs.) in Schutt und Asche legen 9 **tinsel:** Lametta, Flitter **candy cane:** Zuckerstange, klassische amerikanische Weihnachtsdekoration **to block:** verdecken 12 **the projects:** Sozialwohnungsanlage 15 **to plead:** flehen, betteln 19 **weary:** müde, erschöpft

stopped, but there was still lots of shouting. "Just let me look."

"Oh, okay." Gramma gave in just like I knew she would. "Be quick."

I hurried over to the window and parted the curtains a little. Cold winter air seeped in around the edges of the glass. Outside a crowd of people had gathered in the dark. All I could see were the tops of heads and shoulders.

"Let me go see, Gramma," I begged. "I'll stay right by the front, I promise."

"No."

"I ain't gonna get hurt with all those people out there."

Gramma let out a defeated sigh. "You ain't gonna stop botherin' me till I say yes, are you? Come back quick, you hear? And don't go nowhere else."

I grabbed my coat, went down the stairs, and through the dented metal doors to the outside. Cold, dark air filled my lungs. The first kid I saw was Lightbulb, walking in a circle behind the crowd with his eyes squeezed

6 **to seep in:** hereinziehen 13 **ain't:** ugs. für "will not"
16 **to bother s.o.:** jmd. nerven 19 **dented:** verbeult

shut and his fingers in his ears. He was wearing a wool cap and a ratty old man-size coat that dragged on the ground.

"What's goin' on?" I asked.

Lightbulb opened his eyes, but shook his head and kept his fingers in his ears. He'd gotten his nickname because of how light his skin was and the shape of his head. Sometimes he wasn't right in the head, either.

"A shorty fell out a window." Lightbulb winced as if just talking about it caused him pain. "Long way down. He's dead for sure."

By the age of twelve I'd already seen my share of dead folks. The gangbanger lying glassy-eyed in a pool of blood in the lobby. The lady who was stabbed and crawled down four flights of stairs before she bled out. The crusty old wino who froze to death on a bench. But I'd never seen a dead kid before.

The crowd was packed tight. No way a kid my size could fight through all those legs and hips to see. Besides, the police were pushing people back and lining the area with yellow crime scene tape. I decided the best

2 **ratty:** abgerissen, gammelig 9 **shorty:** „Kurzer", kleines Kind **to wince:** zusammenzucken 14 **lobby:** Eingangshalle 16 **crusty:** (ugs.) dreckig, stinkend **wino:** (ugs.) Penner, Alkoholabhängiger 21 **crime scene tape:** Klebeband zur Markierung eines Verbrechensschauplatzes

place to watch was from the monkey bars in the middle of the yard.

The bars were cold against my bare hands. On top I was above the crowd and could see all around. On three sides of us rose the broad buildings of the Frederick Douglass Projects. Lights glowed in some windows and red and green Christmas lights were strung across a few balconies, but more windows were boarded up or broken and dark than bright.

The police had cleared a semi-circle of space against the building, and the ambulance guys were in there, crouching down. Behind me a car door slammed. I turned and saw a black Mercedes with dark windows at the curb, the shiny chrome rims spinning like it was still going a hundred miles an hour. The crowd began to part as someone walked toward the building. He was shorter than some men, but stocky and powerfully built. I couldn't see his face in the dark, but it didn't matter. There was only one person who commanded that kind of respect: Marcus Elliot, the leader of the Douglass Disciples.

1 **monkey bars:** Klettergerüst 8 **boarded up:** mit Brettern zugenagelt 14 **curb:** Bürgersteigkante **rim:** Felge 17 **stocky:** stämmig, von kräftiger Statur 20 **disciple:** Jünger

As usual, Marcus was dressed in black. The crowd quieted down and even the police stepped aside. Marcus stopped in the semi-circle and looked down over the shoulders of the ambulance guys. He stood there for a long time.

The monkey bars creaked as Lightbulb climbed up beside me. His pants were torn at the knees, and the sleeves of his big coat hung down past his hands. He started rocking back and forth, mumbling, "They say it was one of the Gangstas."

The Gangstas were the enemies of the Disciples. They lived a few blocks away, in the Gentry Projects.

One of the ambulance guys went out through the crowd and returned with something long and black.

"What's that?" Lightbulb whispered.

"Body bag," I whispered back. "Go see who it was. Climb down and ask around."

"No way."

"For a Snickers bar," I tempted him.

"Lemme see."

"It's upstairs. I'll give it to you tomorrow."

9 **to rock back and forth:** sich hin und her wiegen
16 **body bag:** Leichensack 20 **Lemme see:** (ugs. für "Let me see") Zeig's mir, will ich sehen

"How do I know you really got one?"

"Leftover from Halloween," I said. "I know where Gramma hides 'em."

"How do I know you gonna keep your word?" Lightbulb asked.

I gave him the look I'd seen on men's faces on TV when their word was on the line. "I ever lie to you?"

"No, not you."

"Well, I ain't lyin' now."

Lightbulb climbed down and disappeared into the crowd. Meanwhile, the ambulance guys lifted the body bag onto a stretcher and rolled it through the crowd. Marcus walked behind them with his head down. The body bag was mostly flat, except for a bump in the middle. It reminded me of a TV show I once saw where a big python swallowed a pig.

As they passed the monkey bars, Marcus glanced up. His face was hard and flat. Jaws clenched, lips tight. Not a handsome face, but one that said he wasn't scared of anyone and anything. The way his eyes were, I wasn't sure he even saw me.

2 **leftover:** Rest 3 **'em:** ugs. für "them" 12 **stretcher:** Trage (hier: mit Rädern) 18 **clenched:** zusammengebissen

Lightbulb climbed back up. “It was Darnell.”

Darnell was Marcus’s little nephew. I twisted back toward Abernathy Avenue. They’d opened the rear ambulance door to slide in the stretcher. The light from inside the ambulance reflected on the men’s faces. You might have expected that Marcus would be looking down at the dead little boy. But he wasn’t. He was staring back at the project with a look as cold and angry as I’d ever seen.

Two

Darnell's momma was Laqueta, Marcus's sister and my best friend Terrell's first cousin. I didn't know who Darnell's daddy was, only that Laqueta's new boyfriend was Jamar, the Disciples' second in command. Everyone said Laqueta was the prettiest girl in the projects, light-skinned with big round eyes and straight white teeth and always a smile. At least, till Darnell was pushed off the roof by the Gentry Gangstas.

Jamar told the police that he had left Darnell on his own for a while. On his return he had found the apartment door open and Darnell gone. He'd searched for him everywhere, but couldn't find him. Two guys came running down the staircase leading to the roof. Jamar hadn't seen it clearly but was pretty sure they wore green

8 **momma:** ugs. für "mother" 9 **first cousin:** Cousine (ersten Grades) 11 **second in command:** stellvertretender Anführer

bandanas, the color of the Gentry Gangstas. When Jamar had run upstairs and onto the roof to look for Darnell he had heard people screaming that a small boy had fallen off.

The next morning, Gramma made me dress in a heavy coat, gloves, and a hat before I could take my bike outside. Despite the cold, it was fun to ride my bike because the ground was hard and you could go almost anywhere in the project. Not like in the spring when the yard was soft and muddy. Something lay on the ground about thirty feet from the yellow crime scene taped spot where Darnell fell, just far enough away that it might have been missed in the crowds and dark the night before. I stopped. It was a window guard, bent in the middle, as if someone had kicked it out of a window frame.

"That where the little boy fell?" a voice behind me asked.

It was a girl with big, pretty eyes. She was wearing a clean pink jacket with a hood lined with white fur. With the hood pulled tightly around her face, she reminded me of an Eskimo.

1 **bandana:** Halstuch, um die Stirn getragen 6 **hat:** Mütze
14 **window guard:** Sicherungsbügel für ein Fenster
20 **hood:** Kapuze

"No, over there." I pointed toward the yellow tape.

"It's so sad," she shivered.

A dozen yards away, out in the bright sunlight, was a bench. I walked my bike toward it and told the girl my name. The wooden seat part of the bench was busted, so I hopped up on the top. The sun was bright and strong and took some of the icy sting out of the air.

"Okay, Kalon. I'm Precious. How old are you?" she asked, her hands in the pockets of her pink jacket.

"Twelve."

"Me, too."

"So where'd a pretty girl like you get a nice jacket like that?" I asked, with the confident smile I'd been practicing in the mirror.

"My daddy gave it to me for Christmas," Precious stated in a self-satisfied sort of way. Having a father at home, and a gift-giving father, too, was a big deal.

"Christmas ain't till next week."

"I got it early 'cause it's cold and I don't have another jacket to wear."

My best friend Terrell Blake came out with his bike.

5 **busted:** kaputt, vandalisiert 13 **confident:** selbstsicher

He rode with one hand, his other jammed down into the hoody's pocket. He was taller than me, with skin a little lighter and a thinner nose. One of his front teeth was chipped from a rock fight.

"How come they let you out?" I asked, knowing he was supposed to be inside with his family grieving over his little nephew Darnell.

"It's too sad and stuffy up there," he said. "Makes my asthma act up." He straddled his bike and eyed my new friend.

"This is Precious," I told him. "She lives in Number Three."

No. 3 was the building across the yard from ours, which was No. 1. Until that year, my friends and I had pretty much stuck close to our own building, too scared to venture far because we might get caught in the crossfire of gangs shooting. But now we were older and more daring.

Out on Abernathy Avenue, Marcus's Mercedes pulled up to the curb. It was rare to see gangbangers around this early in the day. The leader of the Disciples got out

2 **hoody:** Kapuzenshirt 6 **to grieve:** trauern 8 **stuffy:** stickig
16 **to venture:** sich hinauswagen 18 **daring:** wagemutig

and looked around warily, as if half expecting an ambush. But the yard was mostly empty. It was too cold for most people to want to be outside.

Marcus started toward us. Terrell straightened up and I felt myself grow tense. There were no clues in Marcus's expression. It was intense and serious all the time. You never saw him joking or clowning. As he got close, I saw the small tattoo of a tear at the corner of his right eye. For people on the outside, the tear was supposed to mean someone close to you had been killed. But we in the projects knew different – that tear really meant you'd killed someone.

"Uh, hi, cousin Marcus." Terrell's voice quavered.

Marcus barely acknowledged the greeting. "Watch my car," he said, and might have continued toward No. 1, except that I told him there was something I thought he'd want to see. Scowling doubtfully, he started with me toward the building. Terrell got on his bike and followed until Marcus swung around. "I tell you to come?" he asked sharply.

Without a word Terrell rode back to the bench. In the

1 **warily:** misstrauisch, vorsichtig **ambush:** (Angriff aus dem) Hinterhalt 5 **tense:** angespannt 13 **to quaver:** zittern 17 **to scowl:** grimmig dreinschauen

cold shadow of the building, Marcus picked up the window guard and stared up at the highest floors of the building where Laqueta lived with Jamar and Darnell.

Then he looked at me. “Kalon, right? Raven’s son?”

“Yes, sir.”

He tapped the window guard against his palm.

“Knew I’d want to see it?”

“Uh huh.”

Holding the ends in his hands, Marcus slowly squeezed the window guard until it doubled over. The skin of his dark hands tightened and his knuckles bulged. The metal creaked until it formed a V, like the V in the furrows of skin between his eyes as he fixed them on me. “Know what happens to kids who snitch to the police?”

“Uh huh.”

“Know what happens to the families of kids who snitch?”

“Sure I do. But what about Darnell?”

“I’ll take care of it my way,” Marcus said. “Meanwhile, this is our secret.”

6 **palm:** Handfläche 11 **to bulge:** hervortreten, dick werden
12 **furrow:** Furche, Falte 14 **to snitch:** jmd. oder etw. verpfeifen

Three

"Who was that?" Precious asked when I got back to the bench.

Her eyes widened when we told her. "Are you Disciples?"

"Not yet," Terrell answered.

Precious shivered and hugged herself. Even in the sun, the cold gradually seeped through your clothes. "You want to come to my place and watch TV?" she asked.

It was tempting. Neither Terrell nor I had ever been invited in a girl's home, but we couldn't. We had a car to watch.

"Maybe another time," I said.

Precious's soft pretty lips turned down. "Okay, see you later."

13 **to shiver:** frösteln 16 **tempting:** verlockend

Terrell and I rode around the yard, always keeping Marcus's car in sight. I asked him how Laqueta was and he said she'd cried all night.

"Jamar stay with her?" I asked.

Terrell shook his head. He got off his bike and started sliding around on a frozen puddle, leaving white scratches in the dirty, brownish ice.

"If I grow up I'm gonna have a car like that," Terrell said through chattering teeth. He must've been freezing, wearing only that hoody. "And chains and bling like you wouldn't believe. Rance got a solid gold chain that weighs five pounds."

"How do you know that?" I asked. Rance Jones was the leader of the Gentry Gangstas, the rival gang from the Gentry Projects. To us he was just a name and a reputation. I'd never actually seen the man, and I was pretty sure Terrell hadn't either.

"I heard from someone," Terrell said. "And he got a twenty-five carat diamond pinky ring, too. The Gentry Gangstas use kids nine, ten years old."

"Maybe you should join the Gangstas," I joked.

9 **to chatter:** klappern 10 **bling:** (ugs.) Klunker, auffälliger Schmuck 19 **pinky:** kleiner Finger

Terrell jumped off his bike. "Marcus is my cousin," he said proudly. "He should let me join the Disciples."

"And get jumped in?" I asked. To prove you'd be loyal to the gang you had to let yourself be beaten up and burned with cigarettes.

The smile left Terrell's lips. "Everybody else been through it."

We sat on the bench, teeth chattering, watching the dirty city buses and gypsy cabs on Abernathy Avenue. A police cruiser stopped behind Marcus's car. The window went down and Officer Patterson wagged a thick brown finger at us. He was the only person I'd ever heard of who'd grown up in Frederick Douglass and became a cop. I hopped off the bench and went to see what he wanted.

"How you doin', Kalon?" he asked. He had a round face and a thick, bushy moustache. Growing up he'd known my mother, and he always said hello when he saw me.

"Okay." I leaned in the open window. The car smelled like coffee. A shotgun and a computer were mounted

3 **to get jumped in:** die Einführungsrituale über sich ergehen lassen
9 **gypsy cab:** unlizenziertes Taxi 10 **police cruiser:** Streifenwagen
11 **to wag:** hin und her wackeln, wedeln 21 **to mount:** anbringen, befestigen

next to the driver's seat. Officer Patterson nodded at the Mercedes. "Marcus was that little boy's uncle, right?"

"Yes, sir."

"Give him my condolences, okay?"

"What's that?"

"Tell him I'm sorry about his nephew."

"Yes, sir."

Officer Patterson took a sip from a paper cup of coffee and brushed his moustache with the back of his hand. "Kalon means strong warrior, right?"

"That's what my grandma says."

"But you can be a warrior for good, not just bad. You going to join the Disciples someday?"

"No, sir. Gonna stay in school and out of trouble, sir."

"Good boy." Officer Patterson reached over and patted me on the shoulder. Then he drove off and I went back to the bench.

"What do you talk to him for?" Terrell asked.

"He knew my momma."

We sat and watched the traffic. Except for school,

4 **condolences:** Beileid 10 **warrior:** Krieger, Kämpfer

Terrell and I hardly ever left Frederick Douglass. Sometimes I wondered about all those people in all those cars. Where were they all going? How come we didn't have anyplace to go?

"Ahem." Terrell cleared his throat and jerked his head. Marcus was coming toward us. His lips were a hard thin line and his eyes darted toward the Mercedes.

"Anything goin' on?"

"Officer Patterson came by," I said. "Said he was sorry about Darnell."

Marcus's eyebrows dipped ever so slightly. "What else?"

"He asked if I was gonna join the Disciples someday."

The hard, flat line of Marcus's lips began to curl upwards in amusement. "What'd you say?"

I realized I'd made a mistake telling him that. How could I answer?

"I'm ready," Terrell volunteered.

Marcus turned his gaze on him. "You think so?"

5 **to jerk:** eine zuckende Bewegung machen   12 **to dip:** sich senken

Terrell nodded eagerly. “I’ll be your best soulja.”

The gang leader smirked. “Go back inside. Your momma wants you.”

1 **eagerly:** eifrig **soulja:** (ugs. für “soldier”) Soldat, Kämpfer
2 **to smirk:** schief grinsen

Four

The three identical buildings in the Frederick Douglass Projects loomed up like dirty tombstones. The grounds around the buildings were mostly cracked concrete walks covered with broken glass, and hard-packed bare brown dirt with a few trees and some dead brown weeds.

Benches lined the walks, but they were mostly busted. Same with the playground. There were no swings in the swing set, just rusty chains hanging down from the top. The seesaw was gone. What little sand was left in the sandbox was the color of dark smoke. Only the rusty monkey bars remained. As shorties, we used to play on them for hours and then go home with burnt reddish palms.

9 **to loom up:** sich drohend erheben **tombstone:** Grabstein
11 **hard-packed:** festgetreten 13 **weed:** Unkraut
15 **swing:** Schaukel 17 **seesaw:** Wippe

The lobby of our building was lit by one long white flickering bulb and always dim. The mailboxes in the wall had all been busted open by drug fiends looking to steal welfare checks. The walls were covered with colorful loopy graffiti and the black slashes of Disciples' tags.

The elevator was broken as usual so we carried our bikes up the stairs. Some floors smelled of cooking. Other floors smelled of weed. Here and there someone had hung a small Christmas wreath or a bunch of holly outside their door. On some floors you heard loud TV. On others, rap and hip hop. And always in the winter, the banging of the heat pipes day and night like a prison gang eternally busting stone.

Taped on the walls at each landing were blue sheets of paper saying that Darnell's funeral would be at 1 pm on Saturday at the First Baptist Church.

Leaving my bike in my apartment, I went upstairs with Terrell.

On the sixth floor the door to the Blake's apartment was open and inside it was hot and crowded with grown-

2 **dim:** düster 3 **drug fiend:** Drogenabhängiger
4 **welfare:** Sozialhilfe 5 **loopy:** geschwungen **slash:** scharfe, kantige Linie 6 **tag:** Erkennungszeichen einer Gang
9 **weed:** Hasch 10 **wreath:** Kranz **holly:** Stechpalmenzweige
13 **prison gang:** Sträflingskolonne

ups. On a table in the middle of the living room were plates of food and vases of flowers. It was getting toward the end of the month and for a lot of people, food was running low. That was especially true around Christmas when there were presents to buy. When someone died, however, everyone scraped together what little they had to show their sympathy. The sight and smell of those heaping plates made my stomach growl.

Terrell's cousin Laqueta was sitting in the middle of the couch, wearing an old yellow house dress and clutching a tissue. Her eyes were puffy and red from crying. Terrell's momma, Mrs. Blake, sat on one side of her and his aunt Rosa sat on the other.

Jamar sat on a chair nearby with his elbows on his knees and his head hanging. He was tall and rangy. He had the biggest hands and longest fingers I'd ever seen. His hands looked pretty cool with the gold rings and tattoos. Jamar was the Disciples' enforcer, the second in command of the gang. He had a tear tattoo beside his eye.

When Mrs. Blake saw her son, she held open her arms

8 **to heap:** auftürmen 11 **tissue:** Taschentuch
15 **rangy:** langgliedrig 18 **enforcer:** Vollstrecker, Durchsetzer

wide. Terrell hesitated and glanced around as if embarrassed to be treated like a little boy. But then he stepped forward and let her hug him. “Terrell,” she said in a low voice. “You’re the only good man that’s left.”

She looked over Terrell’s shoulder at Jamar when she said that. Laqueta’s boyfriend raised his head and blinked hard, as if trying to squeeze out tears that weren’t there. “If only I didn’t leave Darnell alone,” he said woefully.

People heard him, but no one said anything. If Jamar was hoping someone would try to console him, he was mistaken.

7 **to blink:** blinzeln 8 **woefully:** trübsinnig
11 **to console s.o.:** jmd. trösten

Five

During the day the cops and housing police might come around once in a while, but as soon as it got dark, they were gone. Sometimes gangbangers shot at cops at night. They dropped broken TVs on patrol cars or threw bottles out the windows at them. They didn't need a reason.

If Gramma had her way, I'd be a house boy – only allowed outside to walk to and from school. She would have kept me in the apartment all summer and weekends and everyday after school if she could.

That night Gramma was watching a comedy on the TV. I was on the floor playing an old Gameboy I'd found in the garbage. Gramma laughed so hard she had to take the tissue out of her sleeve and dab her eyes.

21 **to dab:** abtupfen

"How can you laugh at that?" I asked her. "You've seen that show a hundred times."

"I need something to make me laugh," Gramma said, still jiggling. "After what happened to that little boy."

Outside, shooting started. It sounded more like cap guns than the big bangs you heard on the TV. *Pop! Pop! Pop!* You might have thought someone was setting off firecrackers.

Next thing I knew, Gramma was down on the floor next to me. She raised her head alertly. "Where's Nia?" she asked even though we both knew she was with Denzel.

Pop! Pop! Crash! More shots and somewhere nearby a window shattered. *Bang.* A door closed downstairs and we heard rapid steps coming up. A key jiggled in the lock and Nia rushed in. She was breathing hard and her eyes gleamed with excitement.

"Get down!" Gramma commanded.

Still gasping for breath, Nia dropped to one knee, but no lower.

"You're gonna get yourself killed someday," Gramma

4 **to jiggle:** schütteln (hier: vor Lachen) 5 **cap gun:** Pistole mit Platzpatronen

muttered even as she relaxed, knowing that Nia was safe.

"Those boys shoot all the time," Nia scoffed.

"You forget how your momma died?" Gramma snapped. "How many times I have to tell you not to run when they shoot? You hear shooting, you drop to the ground and stay there."

"And get my clothes all dirty? Nuh uh." My sister shook her head.

We waited until the shooting stopped. The TV was still on and the laugh track called Gramma back to the couch. Nia flopped down and put her left arm around Gramma's neck, while she picked up the clicker with her right hand and changed the channel to a rap show.

Pop! Pop! Pop! The shooting started again, but now it sounded far away. Gramma stiffened, but then looked at Nia and me and relaxed. We were safe. At least for tonight.

1 **to mutter:** grummeln, murmeln 3 **to scoff:** spotten, abfällig bemerken 5 **to snap:** fauchen, eine scharfe Bemerkung machen

Six

Gramma's apartment had one bedroom with one bed, which Nia and Gramma shared. I slept on the living room couch. The couch smelled bad. We'd been eating on it, and spilling food on it, for years, and at least once some drunk boyfriend of Gramma's puked all over it.

Most mornings Gramma left to clean houses before we woke up. After breakfast Nia and I washed the dishes. Nia always wore yellow rubber gloves. On TV people had kitchens with dishwashers and bathrooms with showers, but all we had were sinks and a bathtub. Sometimes I'd go into the bathroom and find Gramma on her knees, washing clothes in the tub. For a short time there had been three washing machines in the basement but they broke down after only a few weeks.

12 **to puke:** (ugs.) kotzen

Terrell and Lightbulb were waiting in the yard. In the shadows where Darnell fell, someone had stuck a small wooden cross in the ground, with candles and small bunches of flowers around it. The yellow crime scene tape lay twisted and trampled into the dirt and weeds. The three of us stared at the cross without speaking. Then Lightbulb said, "You got that Snickers bar?"

I gave it to him and he tore it open while we walked to school.

"That your breakfast, Lightbulb?" Terrell teased.

"So?" A bite of Snickers made a bulge in his cheek.

Nia and her boyfriend Denzel walked ahead of us. They were both in eighth grade. Denzel was slim with light chocolate skin and almond-shaped eyes as if he had some Asian blood. A black bandana poked out of his back pocket.

Ahead of us Denzel kissed Nia and then stopped. "Terrell," he called. "Comere."

Terrell practically bounded over. He and Denzel went behind some parked cars. When they came back, Terrell was arranging the front of his hoody.

10 **to tease:** hänseln 13 **eighth grade:** achte Klasse
18 **comere:** ugs. für "Come here" 19 **to bound:** einen Satz machen

"What'd he give you?" I asked as we started walking again.

"Nothing," Terrell answered, his eyes darting this way and that.

"Get lost, Lightbulb."

"Why?" Lightbulb frowned.

"'cause I said so," said Terrell, lowering his voice, as if whatever Denzel had given him suddenly made him a tough street hustler.

Lightbulb hunched his shoulders like his feelings were hurt, then went off. When he was far enough away, Terrell opened the pocket of his hoody a little. Inside was the gray handle of a box cutter.

"Are you whack?" I hissed.

"I'm just gonna bring it inside and give it back," Terrell replied.

"They find it, you'll get expelled."

Terrell shrugged. "No matter ..."

"And what do you think Denzel's gonna do with it in school?" I asked.

"I don't care. All I know is Denzel said he'd put in

9 **street hustler:** Straßenkämpfer 13 **box cutter:** Teppichmesser
14 **whack:** (ugs.) bescheuert, von allen guten Geistern verlassen
17 **to get expelled:** der Schule verwiesen werden

a good word for me to Marcus. Know what that means?"

"Sure, Terrell, I know what that means."

Our school was named Washington Carver after George Washington Carver, a famous African-American scientist. It was on the border between the Frederick Douglass Project and the Gentry Street Project. To the school's builders that must've made sense because kids from both projects could go. But it also put the school right in the middle of the war zone between the Douglass Disciples and the Gentry Gangstas.

Washington Carver had more metal bars around it than a jail. Bars in the tall metal fence that circled the building. Bars over the filthy gray windows. Bars across the doors at the entrances. At Washington Carver the sixth graders went in a different entrance than the seventh and eighth graders, whose bags were scanned and bodies were sometimes searched.

At the sixth grade entrance, Ms. Rodriguez, the assistant principal, watched us enter. She was as ancient as

20 **assistant principal:** stellvertretende Schulleiter(in)
21 **ancient:** uralt

the history we were learning. Her short nappy hair was completely white, and she was all wrinkled skin and bone and gristle. Her job in the morning was to make sure only kids who went to Washington Carver entered, and not any trouble makers from anyplace else.

While we waited on line, I could hear Terrell begin to wheeze. He took out his inhaler and breathed in deep. Then it was our turn to go in. At the doorway, Ms. Rodriguez narrowed her eyes at Terrell, whose hands were both jammed into the pocket of his hoody.

"Wait a minute, young man," she said. "What do you have there?"

1 **nappy:** kraus 3 **gristle:** Knorpel 7 **to wheeze:** keuchen
inhaler: Inhaliergerät

Seven

Terrell began to tremble.

"I –" my friend sputtered anxiously.

"Don't give me no explanations," Ms. Rodriguez snapped. "Just show me what's in that pocket."

Still trembling, Terrell slowly drew his hand from his pocket.

In it was his inhaler.

Ms. Rodriguez's expression softened immediately. "You okay, honey?"

Terrell nodded and she waved him in.

Inside, he grinned at us. "Thought I was gonna get busted, right?"

"So did you," I said.

He shook his head. "Naw, I was just foolin' around."

9 **to sputter:** stottern, ausstoßen **anxiously:** ängstlich, nervös
18 **to get busted:** geschnappt werden 21 **naw:** ugs. für "no"
to fool around: Quatsch machen

He made a right and went down the hall toward the cafeteria.

"Where's he going?" Lightbulb asked.

"Nowhere good," I said.

Inside Washington Carver, everything broken was held together with tape. The cracks in the grimy windows were covered with tape. The bottom of the pull down screen in the front of the room was taped. The pages in the tattered old books we read were held in with tape.

The only things new at school were the teachers. Every year at least half the faces were different.

Take Mr. Brand for example. He was teaching us history. He spoke proper, not ghetto, and wore button-down shirts and slacks with cuffs and was about as white as a black man could be. He was average height, but real thin because, he said, he ran marathons.

"Settle down, everyone," he said at the beginning of class. "Open your text books to page two hundred and eighty-five. Who can tell me why the pyramids were built?"

7 **tape:** Klebeband **grimy:** schmutzig
8 **pull down screen:** Projektionsfläche 10 **tattered:** zerfleddert
14 **proper:** richtig, hier: korrektes Englisch
button-down shirts: Hemden mit festgeknöpften Kragenecken
15 **slacks:** Stoffhosen **cuffs:** Aufschläge

The chubby Douglass kid we called Bublz raised his hand. "Hey, Mr. Brand, is the reason you like ancient history so much because the Egyptians ran marathons like you do?"

"The Greeks ran marathons, not the Egyptians," Mr. Brand replied patiently.

"My book ain't got a page two-hundred eighty-five," complained a girl named Ikea.

"Then share with someone else," said Mr. Brand.

"Hey!" said a big, tough Gentry boy named Antwan, "I didn't know them Egyptians were brothers!"

"What'd you think, dumbass?" said Bublz. "They come from Africa."

"No, they don't," said Antwan. "They come from Egypt. That's why they're called Egyptians, stupid."

"You stupid," Bublz shot back. "Where you think Egypt is?"

"In Egypt, retard," said Antwan. "And Africa's in Africa."

Bublz shook his head wearily. "If you were any dumber they'd have to give you a brain transplant."

1 **chubby:** dicklich 11 **brothers:** Brüder (hier: Schwarze)
12 **dumbass:** Arschgesicht 18 **retard:** Vollidiot
20 **dumber:** blöder

Bublz and Antwan were engaged in the daily ritual of clowning, seeing how far they could go and how much class time they could waste before Mr. Brand got angry. After a while Mr. Brand smartened up and learned that if he let the class mess around for a while, they might get bored and eventually let him teach. Some days it worked, some days it didn't. A week like this, before a big vacation like Christmas was pretty much a lost cause.

In a moment of quiet Mr. Brand saw a chance to step in. "Who can tell Antwan the difference between Egypt and Africa?"

A couple of hands went up, including mine.

"Kalon?" Ms. Brand called.

"Africa's a continent," I said. "Egypt's a country in Africa."

"Where in Africa?" asked Mr. Brand.

"Like north Africa."

"Well, look at the brains on Kalon," Antwan said snidely. "Maybe I'll kick your Douglass ass."

Instead of answering, I gave him the steely look I ima-

4 **to smarten up:** etw. kapieren 5 **to mess around:** Mist machen
8 **lost cause:** aussichtsloser Fall 20 **snide:** abfällig

gined Marcus would use. Only, I wondered if Marcus's heart ever beat as hard as mine did at that moment.

"What's that?" Antwan taunted. "You trying to look tough? You about as tough as my baby sister."

"I said, that's enough," said Mr. Brand. But it didn't matter now. The class was waiting for my response. There was no backing down. Not unless you wanted to be called soft, and get picked on constantly.

"I'll see you after school," I muttered.

The class oohed and ahhed.

Antwan narrowed his eyes and nodded as if he accepted the challenge. Meanwhile Terrell gave me a nod and made a fist under his desk. We were sworn to watch each other's backs.

Class ended. As I headed for the door, Mr. Brand said, "Hold on, Kalon."

I waited while the others left.

My teacher gave me a searching look. "Are you really going to fight him?"

"If I have to, sir." The truth was, most of the talk was just bluster to be forgotten as soon as the bell rang.

3 **to taunt s.o.:** jmd. verspotten 7 **to back down:** nachgeben
8 **to pick on s.o.:** es auf jmd. abgesehen haben
21 **bluster:** heiße Luft

Mr. Brand shook his head as if it made no sense. "Tell me something, Kalon. Why do they even bother coming to class?"

"Nothing better to do," I said.

"What about you?"

Gramma said I was a good boy because I did what I was told. But most of the time I only did that because it was easier than not doing it. I had a pretty good notion that school wasn't the way to succeed. We'd all heard stories about the rich and famous rappers like *50 Cent* and *Athletes* who'd come from the projects. But you never heard about anyone from the projects who got famous for being smart.

Mr. Brand tapped the eraser of a pencil against his desk. "Have you ever heard of the Hewlett School, Kalon?"

"No, sir."

"It's a special school over in Beech Hill for kids who deserve a chance," he said. "You'll get a better education there."

"Beech Hill's far," I said a little nervously.

8 **s.o. has a notion:** jmd. ist etwas klar

"You could take a bus." I guess he could tell that I wasn't thrilled by the idea. "Don't want to leave your friends, right? Don't want to leave the comfort and familiarity of the 'hood."

I nodded.

"Kalon, what do you think's going to happen if you stay here?"

"Go to Munson High, I guess."

"You know that more than half the kids who enter there don't finish?"

"Doesn't mean I won't be one of them," I said.

Mr. Brand's shoulders sagged as if pulled down by the weight of something he knew that I didn't.

"Kalon, listen to me. It's one thing to go to school here with all your friends. But it's different when your crew's dropped out and you're the only one left. It's different when you're still walking to school each day while your peeps drive around with plenty of bling in hot rides. You can understand that, right?"

I nodded again. The second bell rang. It was lunchtime and I started inching toward the door.

4 **'hood:** (eigtl.: neighborhood) Nachbarschaft 12 **to sag:** sinken
18 **peeps:** (ugs. Abk. für "people") Leute **hot ride:** dickes Auto
21 **to inch toward:** sich langsam auf etw. zubewegen

"Wait," Mr. Brand said. "I want you to think about Hewlett, okay? It's still two years away, but there are things you could start doing to prepare. There's a special Saturday program I could help you get into."

"I'll think about it."

He gazed thoughtfully at me. "You're pretty good at telling people what they want to hear, aren't you?"

I looked into his eyes. He was the only black person with green eyes that I'd ever seen.

"You're probably wondering why I even bother, right?" Mr. Brand asked. I nodded.

"What I've started to realize is that most of these kids don't want my help. They're perfectly happy to waste their days clowning around without a thought about the future. But maybe you're different. You're one of the few in this class who reads at grade level. Maybe you're the one who'll really do something with his life. But to do that you'll need a better education than you'll get here. So you'll think about Hewlett, right?"

I nodded. He placed the pass in my hand and I headed for the door.

16 **at grade level:** der Klassenstufe entsprechend

Eight

Just before the end of school they announced a delayed dismissal and all sixth graders were sent to the gym. This happened about once a month, usually because there was going to be a gang fight after school and the school found out and called the police.

"You think that's why Denzel brought that box cutter?" Terrell asked as we walked down the hall to the gym.

"Shhh!" I pressed my finger to my lips. You never knew who might be listening. In the gym kids were standing around in groups or sitting in circles on the floor. Lightbulb sat down and took out a book and a thick pair of old-man eyeglasses with big brown frames.

"Since when do you need glasses to read?" I asked.

9 **dismissal:** Unterrichtsende

He shrugged. "They make me look smart."

"You look dumb in those things," Terrell said. "Ain't nothin' gonna make you look smart."

"Says you," replied Lightbulb.

"What's a hundred and forty-five times two hundred and sixteen?" Terrell asked.

Lightbulb closed his eyes and moved his lips. "Thirty-one thousand, three hundred and twenty."

"That right?" Terrell looked at me.

"How would I know?" I said.

Lightbulb read for a while, then took off the glasses and pressed his fingers into the corners of his eyes. "My head hurts."

"Where'd you get those glasses?" I asked.

"Found 'em."

"You can't just wear any old pair of glasses," I said. "You have to go to a doctor and get them made special."

"For real?" Lightbulb looked at me with his big brown eyes. Some teachers said Lightbulb was a genius. He may have been a genius in school, but in some ways he really was the dumbest kid we knew.

"Hey, Kalon." Terrell nudged me with his elbow. "Someone's checkin' you out."

A group of giggling girls was sitting in a circle across the way. One was taller than the others with long brown hair and sparkling eyes. She was the one Terrell was talking about. We'd been exchanging looks for a few weeks.

"Which one?" Lightbulb asked eagerly.

"Tall one," said Terrell.

Lightbulb was clearly impressed. "She's real pretty."

I felt Terrell's elbow in my side again. "Go talk to her."

"Back off."

"You scared?"

"No."

"Then go."

The truth was, I did want to go. I felt drawn to that tall pretty girl the way Lightbulb was drawn to candy.

The girls around the tall one grew jumpy with excitement, and began whispering in her ear. Her eyes widened and then a faint scowl appeared on her face. Suddenly it

1 **to nudge s.o.:** jmd. anstoßen 13 **back off:** Lass mich in Ruhe
19 **jumpy:** nervös 21 **faint:** schwach, leicht

seemed as if she was annoyed with their chatter, because she got up and came toward me.

"Go on, get closer," one of her friends called and the others cackled.

The tall girl turned to them. "Shush! Shut your mouths." She spoke with authority, and the other girls actually got quiet. I liked that.

"I'm Kalon." I introduced myself.

"I know," she said, tilting her head toward the other girls. "They told me. I'm Tanisha."

"New here?"

She nodded. Her eyes were glowing.

"Where're you from?" I asked.

"The east side. We moved over the summer."

"Like it here?" I asked.

The glow left her eyes. "This is a bad neighborhood. I liked it better where I was."

"How come you moved?" I asked.

She lowered her head and stared at the ground. The reasons for moving to the projects were never good.

"Sorry," I said. "That's none of my business."

4 **to cackle:** gackernd lachen 9 **to tilt:** neigen

She raised her head. "How long've you been around here?"

"All my life. My gramma moved here about thirty years ago."

"Your momma go to this school?"

"Yeah."

"Bet she had Ms. Rodriguez," she said. "She's so old, *everybody* must've had her."

I laughed. "Where do you live now?"

"Gentry," she said.

Everything went from hot to cold. From hope to no hope. It didn't matter that I wasn't a Disciple. I was from Frederick Douglass and if I got seen by Gentry Gangstas on their turf, they would automatically consider me a spy and up to no good. They might not kill me for that, but I was sure to catch a beating.

Tanisha frowned. She must've sensed something was wrong.

"Well, nice to meet you," I said, and turned away.

14 **turf:** Territorium, Gelände 17 **to sense:** spüren

Nine

Gramma gave me a blue knitted sweater for Christmas that I definitely wouldn't ever wear. I had gotten Nia and her two small bottles of perfume from the street vendor. We had chicken for lunch and then I left to meet Lightbulb.

"Where're we going?" Lightbulb asked as we met in the hall.

"Upstairs," I said.

Lightbulb stopped. "You crazy? No one but Disciples are allowed up there."

"Shh ... Quiet. I need a look out."

"Who's gonna look out for me?" Lightbulb asked as we climbed the piss-smelly stairwell.

"I got a Snickers bar."

10 **street vendor:** Straßenhändler 18 **look out:** Wachposten
20 **stairwell:** Treppenhaus

We made it to the fifteenth floor. This was Disciples territory. Not that they paid rent. They'd broken through the doors and put on their own locks and used the apartments as places to live and safe houses for anyone who needed to hide.

The stairwell and hallway were covered with loopy tags – *TAP* and *Casper* and *Zig Zag* – and also, everywhere, like religious symbols to ward off evil spirits, the six-pointed star symbol of the Disciples.

Pressed against a wall was an old nicked chest of drawers. It didn't make sense for it to be there and I started to push it aside.

"What're you doing?" Lightbulb whispered.

"Shh ..." Behind the chest was a hole through the cinderblock wall big enough for someone to crawl through. I bent down and peeked into an empty room with a bare mattress lying on the floor. Giving the Snickers bar to Lightbulb, I said, "You hear anyone come up the stairs, you holler into this hole, then go down the other stairs as fast as you can."

Lightbulb was already tearing open the wrapper. He

8 **to ward off:** fernhalten, abwenden 10 **nicked:** abgesplittert, zerkratzt **chest of drawers:** Kommode 14 **cinderblock:** Blähbetonstein 16 **to peek:** spähen 19 **to holler:** rufen

took a bite and nodded. I crawled through the hole. Inside the floor was covered with empty bottles, cigarette butts, magazines and food wrappers. The bare mattress was stained a dozen different shades of yellow and brown. I crossed the room to the door and stopped to listen. It sounded quiet on the other side and I slowly opened the door and went down the hall.

About a million cockroaches scattered when I entered the kitchen. It smelled like garbage, and the sink and counters were covered with dirty dishes, empty take out containers, fried chicken buckets, and pizza boxes. The faucet dripped. I opened the cabinet under the sink and about a million more cockroaches scattered. At the back of the cabinet behind the pipes was another hole. I'd heard that the holes were so gangbangers could escape if the police raided. If you followed the holes through each apartment you eventually came to a stairwell. In some rooms there were even holes in the floors so they could drop down to another floor and escape that way.

I crawled into the next apartment. This one had a strong, chemical smell. In the first room I came to was a

4 **shade:** Farbton 7 **hall:** Flur 8 **cockroach:** Küchenschabe **to scatter:** hastig auseinanderlaufen 10 **counter:** Arbeitsplatte 12 **faucet:** Wasserhahn **cabinet:** Schrank 16 **to raid:** eine Razzia machen

ping pong table and folding chairs. On the table were cutting boards and razor blades smudged with yellowish-white powder, and a couple of small postal scales. Hundreds of small empty zip-lock baggies and clear plastic vials were scattered about.

In the kitchen, piled on the counter and sink, were dozens of empty orange and red boxes of baking soda, and half a dozen old, dented cooking pots. Even at the age of twelve I knew what the postal scales, baggies, and cooking utensils were for.

I had to crawl through two more apartments before I got to the one where Jamar and Laqueta lived. Terrell said that ever since Darnell died, Laqueta was staying with them on the sixth floor. Unlike the other apartments, this one was pretty clean and had windows with curtains and nice furniture and a big TV in the living room. Both windows in the living room had window guards.

The next room had a small bed with brown and green Simba sheets and pillows. Some stuffed animals and toy trucks were on the floor. The window was open and the

2 **smudged:** beschmiert 3 **postal scale:** Briefwaage 4 **zip-lock baggies:** (eigtl. bags) wiederverschließbare Frischhaltebeutel
5 **vial:** Röhrchen 7 **baking soda:** Backpulver
10 **utensils:** Gerätschaften, Utensilien 20 **Simba:** Disneyfigur (Löwe)

blue curtain was half in and half out so I knew there was no window guard. Carefully pulling the curtain back, I stuck my head outside.

Down in the yard people were the size of Tic Tacs, and on the street cars looked like toys. Behind Douglass was a big rail yard with dozens of tracks. On them were silver passenger trains, black or brown freight trains, and livestock and coal carriers. Most just sat there, but a few were moving and I heard the sharp squeak of metal wheels. Between Frederick Douglass and the yard was a double row of tall chain link fence with coils of razor wire on top to keep people from getting into the yard and stealing or writing graffiti. I knew the fence was supposed to keep people out of the rail yard, but it also felt like it was supposed to keep us in.

I looked at the window frame. In the holes that would have held the window guard in place were broken rusty brown screws with shiny silver insides as if they had just recently snapped. To my mind, it would have taken a hard kick to snap those screws.

A lock clacked somewhere in the apartment. I froze.

6 **rail yard:** Eisenbahngelände **track:** Gleis 8 **livestock:** Vieh
9 **squeak:** Quietschen 11 **chain link fence:** Maschendrahtzaun
razor wire: Stacheldraht

The door to the room I was in was open. If someone came down the hall, they'd see me. I ducked down behind a chest of drawers.

Out in the apartment a door creaked and I heard footsteps.

"You got hollow tips?" a voice asked.

"How many you need?" That voice sounded like Jamar's.

"How much are they?"

"Dollar each."

"A dollar? That's robbery!"

"Take it or leave it," said Jamar.

"Ain't no place else to get 'em and you know it," the other voice said angrily. "You got me right where you want me. Riskin' my life to come over here, and you know damn well I can't go back empty-handed."

If Jamar answered, I couldn't hear him. The next thing I heard was the other man say, "I'll take a hundred. And I won't be sorry if one of 'em winds up in the back of your skull."

"Merry Christmas," replied Jamar coldly.

6 **hollow tips:** Hohlspitzgeschosse

A door slammed. I stayed behind the dresser, my breaths short and shallow. Now I was trapped. If I got caught there was a chance I'd be falling fifteen floors, too.

I heard Jamar moving around in the other room, whistling. A drawer opened and shut. Then the door creaked and closed. I heard the lock click.

I waited a few more minutes, then quietly went down the hall. Lying on the living room table was an open black and gold box. Inside were bronze and gray bullets.

Crawling through the holes in apartment walls, I made it back to where I'd left Lightbulb. He was gone. He'd probably heard Jamar and the other guy coming up the stairs, got scared and ran. If any other kid had done that, I would have been mad. But it was hard to be mad at Lightbulb.

15 **to be mad:** wütend sein

Ten

The First Baptist Church was in a storefront on Belmar Street. It had once been a pet store, but there'd been a fire and now it was a church with rows of pews and an altar. On damp days the rancid smell of old smoke still hung in the air, and up near the altar it smelled like those little green pellets you fed pet hamsters and mice.

The Disciples were standing outside. Today they wore suits. Instead of baseball caps they wore gray fedoras. The suits looked new and expensive and I felt ashamed of my ill-fitting Goodwill hand-me-downs. Nia went to Denzel and gave him a kiss, but as I passed the Disciples I kept my eyes down. Then, at the entrance to the church, a hand came out to stop me. I looked up into the hard eyes of Marcus.

8 **storefront:** Ladenzeile 10 **pew:** Kirchenbank 11 **damp:** feucht **rancid:** ranzig 13 **pellets:** Kügelchen 15 **fedora:** breitkrempiger Hut 17 **ill-fitting:** schlecht sitzend **Goodwill:** Wohltätigkeitsladen **hand-me-downs:** abgelegte und weitergereichte Kleidungsstücke

"Where's your tie?"

I pulled it out of my pocket. I had no idea how to tie a tie, but I'd remembered to put one in my pocket this morning.

"Give it here, and turn around."

I did as I was told and felt Marcus press behind me as he reached over and tied my tie. The corner of something hard jutted into my back and I knew at once why all the Disciples had kept their jackets buttoned.

Marcus's hands were quick and sure as he knotted the tie around my neck and tightened it until I thought I'd choke. Then I felt his strong hands on my shoulders and he pointed me toward the church entrance. I didn't dare say anything and quickly went inside.

They'd put Darnell in a small, light blue coffin surrounded by bunches of red and yellow flowers. The coffin was open and people were going up to look. In the front row Laqueta sat next to Mrs. Blake and Terrell, dabbing her eyes with a handkerchief. She turned her head and looked to the back of the church, and I realized she was looking at Jamar. Maybe she wanted him to sit with her.

8 **to jut:** hervorstehen

But Jamar stood in the back with the other Disciples and didn't move.

Terrell's mom whispered in his ear and he stood up and looked back, scanning the crowd until his eyes caught mine. He jerked his head and I knew he wanted me to go with him to look in the coffin. I gave Gramma a questioning glance and she nodded.

Like I said, I'd seen dead people before, but never a shorty. If a shorty could die, then anyone could.

"My little cousin," Terrell whispered under his breath with watery eyes. I put my hand on his shoulder and after a moment we went back to our seats.

Minister Franklin had barely begun his sermon when the first shot was fired. Hardly anyone looked up. Maybe we were all so used to hearing gun fire that at first it didn't mean anything. But louder shots quickly followed. Glass began to crash and some plaster in the wall exploded. Women started screaming. Minister Franklin ducked down behind the pulpit, and Gramma pushed Nia and me down to the floor between the pews.

14 **minister:** Pastor, Geistlicher **sermon:** Predigt
18 **plaster:** Putz 20 **pulpit:** Kanzel

The tiles felt cold and gritty. All around us people were on the floor, their eyes squeezed shut and their good clothes getting dirty and wrinkled. *Pop! Pop! Pop!* We could hear the sharp zings and cracks as bullets whizzed overhead hitting walls and pews.

The shooting stopped. Car tires screeched. Footsteps slapped as some of the men ran outside. I slithered along the floor and stuck my head out into the aisle. The windows at the front of the church were shot out and only big jagged shards remained. Outside on the sidewalk, framed by the doorway, Marcus stood tall, his arm straight out, firing a big black gun with slow deliberateness.

Pop!

Pop!

Pop!

He looked so powerful in his dark suit. Like some TV hero who wasn't afraid of anyone or anything. A few other Disciples had crouched behind cars and lamp posts. Now they came out and joined Marcus.

Inside the church people began to get up. Minister Franklin poked his head out from behind the altar.

1 **gritty:** rau 7 **to slither:** rutschen 8 **aisle:** Gang
10 **jagged:** gezackt **shards:** Glasscherben
12 **deliberateness:** Sorgfalt

"Damn Gangstas," Nia grumbled angrily as she smoothed out her pink dress and brushed the dirt off.

"How do you know?" I asked.

Nia gave me a look like I was stupid. "It's Marcus's nephew in that casket. Besides, who else would shoot up a funeral?"

Heads turned as Marcus came down the aisle, his face squeezed tight with anger. He said something to Minister Franklin and then went outside again.

The minister continued the service. Only now Marcus and the Disciples stood on the sidewalk in case the Gentry Gangstas came back. Cold air filled the church. We pulled our coats on and shivered while Minister Franklin told us how Darnell was with the angels.

THIRTEEN YEARS OLD

Public schools in the United States are becoming more racially segregated, and the trend is likely to accelerate because of a recent Supreme Court decision forbidding most voluntary local efforts to integrate educational institutions.

to accelerate: beschleunigen

Eleven

The projects stayed the same, but I changed. I wouldn't be caught dead in the pants and shirts Gramma got from the Goodwill store. Now I wore baggy jeans and big hoodies and chains like the other guys.

I woke early, and quietly dressed. It wasn't even eight o'clock and already the apartment felt hot. In the kitchen, the cockroaches scattered from the counters and floor when I turned on the light. After wiping a bowl clean in case roaches had crawled on it during the night, I filled it with Corn Flakes and got the milk out of the refrigerator. It smelled awful and came out in lumps when I dumped it down the drain. It was the end of the month. We were out of bread and there wasn't enough powdered milk for a meal. This wouldn't be the first time I'd eat Corn Flakes with water.

I was heading for the front door when Gramma shuffled out of the bedroom.

"Where you goin'?" she said.

"Out."

"No, you ain't. Been too much shooting around here."

"Not during the day."

"Was yesterday," Gramma said. For a moment the day before, shots had rung out across the yard, sending people scurrying for cover. But it ended as fast as it had begun, and the shooters were never seen.

"That was different," I said.

But why did I have to listen to her? Who was she anyway? Just some old woman in a ratty old nighty. Besides, it wasn't like I was going to do anything bad. I just wanted to go outside.

"You don't know what you'll be, child," Gramma said. "But I do."

What answer was there to this? I tried a smile. "Just

12 **to scurry:** hasten, rennen   16 **nighty:** Nachthemd

because I'm goin' out don't mean I'll join the Disciples," I said, pulling the door open.

"Just because you're goin' out don't guarantee you'll come back," Gramma muttered.

I hung my head, unable to look her in the eye, but feeling a pull I couldn't resist. I left without another word.

Outside, the sun was bright and a few people were going to church. Lightbulb was sitting on the back of the bench, writing in a book. A little nappy-haired girl of about five was playing with a doll in front of the bench. She was wearing a stained green jumper and had a lollipop in her mouth.

"Hi, Lollipop," I said.

Lightbulb's sister looked up at me and grinned, some gaps where her baby teeth had fallen out. The lollipop bulged one side of her cheek.

Lightbulb grinned. "I'm watching her till my momma gets back from the store."

I sat next to him and looked over his shoulder. "What's that?"

"Sudokus." He tore out a page from the beginning of the book and gave it to me. The page said *Easy*, but it wasn't. I worked at it for a while, then got tired and stopped. Meanwhile, Lightbulb worked on a puzzle in the *Super Hard* part of the book. Lickity split he filled in each box and in no time had finished and turned to the puzzle on the next page. Someone who didn't know Lightbulb might have assumed he was faking, but he wasn't.

The sun slowly rose and the day grew hotter. Women came out with babies in strollers and sat in whatever shade they could find. Some older guys squatted near a wall playing hip hop on a boom box while they smoked. Lightbulb's momma came back from the store and took Lollipop.

I was happy when I saw Terrell making his way towards us. He slid his earring into his ear and turned the bill of his cap to the right.

"S'up?" he asked.

"Nothin'. Just chillin'."

"Cookin' is more like it," Lightbulb said. By now

5 **lickety split:** im Handumdrehen 11 **stroller:** Kinderwagen
12 **to squat:** hocken 13 **boom box:** Ghettoblaster
19 **S'up?:** (Kurz für "What's up?") Was gibt's? Was geht?

he'd finished all the Super Hard puzzles and was wearing the book, open in the middle, on his head like a hat to keep the sun off.

A car horn honked. A police car had stopped at the curb and inside, Officer Patterson wagged his finger at me. But I didn't move.

Those days were over. Officer Patterson and I exchanged a long look, then he swiveled his head around and drove back into traffic.

Terrell bounced from foot to foot and seemed all jittery, like a dope fiend who can't find a fix. "I got to get out of here," he said. "Sometimes I just can't stand this place one more minute. I mean, look at it. Everything's broken and dead. It's like the last place on Earth."

I knew what he meant. Except for the weeds, the ground was bare and dusty. Pieces of broken glass glittered in the sun, and here and there lay a discarded Pamper. Just a few years ago we'd happily run around and played our games here. It never occurred to us that there was anything wrong. But now it was like we'd grown a new set of eyes.

4 **to honk:** hupen

"Want to take a walk?" I asked.

Terrell shook his head. "Too hot. Wish there was someplace air-conditioned to go."

"The bus," Lightbulb said.

Terrell grinned. "Okay, let's go."

Lightbulb gave me a nervous glance. I knew how he felt. The only times I'd ever gone farther than school was with Gramma and Nia to the emergency room, or court, or the social services office.

"Where?" Lightbulb asked.

"Don't matter," Terrell said. "We'll stay on it till it comes back here."

Lightbulb slid his hands into his pockets. "Ain't got no bus fare."

"Won't need it. Or you a momma's boy?" Terrell taunted him.

Lightbulb looked at me. "You gonna do it, Kalon?"

I nodded, not letting on that I was as nervous as he was.

We waited at the bus stop where Gramma stood in the morning on her way to clean houses. When the bus

8 **emergency room:** Notaufnahme **court:** Gericht

came, Terrell led us in the middle doors where people usually got off. The air conditioning poured over us like a cool welcoming breeze.

The driver was frowning in the rearview mirror.

The bus pulled back into traffic and soon we were in a different world. The Douglass Projects might have been tall buildings, but the rest of the 'hood was all skeevy old bars and stores, abandoned buildings, and vacant lots filled with garbage and debris. Now we traveled through a world where the buildings were twice as high and the streets and sidewalks were filled with people jammed so close that it looked like they were brushing shoulders.

Everything looked shiny and new. The stores had sparkling windows without bars, and doors you could simply walk through without being buzzed in. It seemed impossible that all this existed just a few dozen blocks from where we lived.

"Man, that's a lot of white people!" Lightbulb blurted.

A fat man in another seat chuckled. Lightbulb low-

7 **skeevy:** heruntergekommen 8 **abandoned:** verlassen **vacant:** leer **lot:** Grundstück 9 **debris:** Schutt 15 **bars:** Gitter 16 **to be buzzed in:** mittels eines elektrischen Türöffners eingelassen werden 19 **to blurt:** hervorstoßen 21 **to chuckle:** in sich hineinlachen

ered his voice to a whisper so the man wouldn't hear: "I never knew there was so many."

"There's way more white people than black," Terrell whispered back.

"How do you know?" Lightbulb asked.

"Look at TV," said Terrell.

"There's plenty of blacks on TV," Lightbulb replied.

"Where?" Terrell said. "On Comedy shows? Rap videos? You ever seen *a crowd* on TV? Like at a baseball game? Football game? The Olympics or something? It's all white. The only time you see a crowd of blacks on TV, it's got to be a riot."

Terrell had a point, but I understood what Lightbulb meant, too. Except for TV and the movies, I'd never seen so many white people either.

People got on and off the bus. Some noticed the three black kids squeezed into one seat, but most didn't.

12 **riot:** Aufstand

Twelve

It's strange how so much of what we see and hear in a day gets forgotten, but some things take hold in our minds and refuse to let go. Days later that trip on the bus kept coming back to me. All those tall, clean buildings without bars on the windows or doors. All those people walking around like they had someplace to go. It wasn't that I yearned to be part of that; it still seemed too strange and foreign. I felt as if they'd spot me right away as someone who didn't belong, who didn't know how to act or what to say. They'd shoo me away, or maybe even call the police.

Sure, I'd seen those other worlds on TV. The cribs and fleets of cars that rappers and athletes had, neighborhoods with two-story houses and green lawns, rain

14 **to yearn:** sich sehnen 17 **to shoo s.o. away:** jmd. verscheuchen
19 **crib:** (ugs.) Hütte, Wohnung

forests and jungles and deserts and mountains. But all that was TV, and even though we knew it was real, it was only real in some distant, unreachable way. I felt no more likely to set foot in a rapper's mansion than in the Amazon rainforest.

"Kalon, there any toast and olives?" Nia called from the living room.

Tanisha smiled at me and her eyes twinkled. We were in the kitchen – the only place in the apartment where we could get a little privacy. I opened the fridge and pulled out bread and olives. It was just past the first of the month and Gramma's check and food stamps had arrived, so there was plenty of food.

"She eats all day," Tanisha whispered.

"You would, too," I whispered back.

I headed to the living room where my sister was propped against some pillows on the couch with her hair tied in a dozen little pigtails and her face glistening with a sheen of perspiration. The TV was on loud so she could hear it over the whir of the window fan. Under a big

4 **mansion:** Herrenhaus, große Villa   13 **food stamps:** Essensmarken   18 **to be propped against sth.:** an etw. gelehnt sein
19 **pigtails:** Zöpfe   **to glisten:** glänzen   20 **sheen:** Glanz
perspiration: Schweiß   21 **whir:** Surren   **fan:** Ventilator

white tee shirt her stomach was swollen to the size of a basketball.

"You're a good brother," she said.

"Can I feel?"

My sister gave an irritated groan and nodded. I think she was getting tired of me asking to feel her stomach, but I was fascinated by her pregnancy. As always, she sent me away as soon as I had touched her belly.

I went back to the kitchen. Tanisha looked so cute with her glittering earrings, a white tee shirt, and shorts that showed off her long legs. I didn't like her looking at the clock, though.

"I better go," she said.

"You sure?" I didn't want her to leave. Over the past year, my worries about her being from Gentry had been overcome by my feelings for her. We'd stay after school and talk and hang out, and one thing led to another ... Other girls wore sexier clothes and more make-up. They brushed against me in the school halls and gave me inviting looks. But there was something proud and dignified about Tanisha that they didn't have.

20 **dignified:** würdevoll

"My momma's gonna wonder where I am," she said.

"Just a little longer." I took her in my arms and kissed her.

Tanisha kissed back, but then started to wiggle out of my grasp.

"Lemme go, Kalon," she breathed hotly in my ear. "If I don't get home soon, my momma's gonna start asking questions." While my family knew about Tanisha, she had not told her family about me. And if it wasn't for her brother being big in the Gangstas, it wouldn't be a problem.

As we left the building, Tanisha slid her hand into mine. The afternoon sun had dipped behind No. 3, casting a long shadow across the yard, which was crowded with people escaping from hot, cramped apartments that always felt smaller and more jammed in the summer.

"Hey, lover boy!" Terrell and his new crew were hanging around the bench. There was the fat kid named Bublz, and a kid a year younger than us named Darius, who was small, but wiry and stronger than he looked. He

4 **to wiggle:** sich winden 13 **to cast:** werfen
15 **cramped:** beengt 21 **wiry:** drahtig

was crazy about hip-hop and thought he would become a big rap star one day. Some guys nicknamed him Darius Slim, making a bad joke that he might end up like the rapper Soulja Slim who was shot dead in New Orleans some years ago.

As Marcus wouldn't let his young cousin become a Disciple, Terrell had decided to start a junior gang of his own. They sold bootleg CDs and DVDs for $3 and $5. As long as they didn't sell drugs or interfere with other Disciple activities, Marcus didn't seem to care.

"Goin' out back?" Terrell yelled with a grin.

"Walking Tanisha back," I said, meaning as far as I could take her without crossing into Gentry territory.

"Let's talk." Terrell jerked his head to the side like some kind of tough guy. The pose annoyed me, but since he was my friend, I gave Tanisha a look that said to wait, then Terrell and I walked out of earshot and stopped near the spot near our building where eight months before Darnell had fallen to his death. All that was left of the shrine was a piece of wood from the cross and the stub of a red candle.

8 **bootleg:** Raubkopie 17 **earshot:** Hörweite

Terrell pulled a toothpick out of his pocket and slid it between his lips. “What’re you doin’ with that Gentry girl?”

“You know her name. Don’t put on this pose with me.”

“Pose?” Terrell shook his head. “This ain’t no pose. Gentry’s the enemy.”

“Wrong. Maybe the Disciples’ enemy, but not ours.”

Terrell shifted the toothpick from one side of his mouth to the other and glared at me. His act was getting on my nerves. “How come you ain’t joined our gang? With you in it we’d be *a force*.”

I glanced at his “crew” around the bench, crossing their arms and lowering their gazes, practicing defiant, menacing looks.

“The only reason you don’t join is because of *her*.”

“The only reason I don’t join is ’cause I don’t *want* to.”

“House boy,” Terrell snarled. It was about as bad an insult as you could fling and I felt my fists ball up in anger and frustration.

4 **to put on:** aufsetzen 10 **act:** Nummer, Pose, Rolle
14 **defiant:** trotzig, widerspenstig 19 **house boy:** Stubenhocker, Muttersöhnchen **to snarl:** knurren, fauchen 20 **to fling an insult at s.o.:** jmd. eine Beleidigung an den Kopf werfen

Terrell lifted his fists. "Come on, let's see what you got."

But his eyes darted back at his crew and I knew it was just more show. I dropped my fists and started back toward Tanisha. Terrell followed me.

"You're messin' everything up for me. If you got with us, Marcus would have to think serious about bringing us into the Disciples."

"How about you get with me and think serious about coming back to Washington Carver?" I asked.

Terrell jerked his head at Tanisha, who was talking on her cell phone, her face bright and animated. "Only reason *you* go is 'cause of her."

I spun around and aimed a finger at his face. "For the last time, you leave her out of this. You get with the gangbangers and all *you're* gonna do is wind up dead or in jail."

"Marcus and Jamar ain't in jail," Terrell replied. "They're wearin' fresh clothes and drivin' hot rides. They got more bank and bling than you'll ever get from goin' to school."

20 **bank:** (ugs.) Kohle, Geld

I turned and headed toward Tanisha, who snapped her phone shut and gave me an impatient look.

"Come on, Kalon," Terrell said behind me. "You know you gonna join up sooner or later. Around here there ain't nothin' else you can do."

Thirteen

It turned even hotter the next day. Terrell and I were up in his apartment playing Thrill Kill on his X-Box with the window fan blowing on us like a gale. The anger we'd felt the day before had passed, but I wasn't sure that meant our friendship was the same as before. We were both careful not to mention Tanisha. Terrell paused the game and went over to his desk and took a handful of peanuts in the shell out of a plastic bag.

"Want some?"

"Where'd you get 'em?" I cracked a shell open.

"Cousins in Georgia. They got their own farm."

"Ever been there?"

Terrell shook his head. "What do I want to go see some farm for?"

10 **gale:** Sturm

From outside, above the whir of the fan, came yelling and laughter. I went to the window. Someone had opened a fire hydrant on Abernathy and bare-chested boys, and girls in tee shirts were playing in the spray.

"Looks like fun," I said. "Want to get wet?"

"You gonna go down there and play with shorties?" Terrell asked derisively, sitting in front of the TV screen, his hands working feverishly, his forehead glistening with sweat.

"Who cares?" I said. "Long as we cool off?"

Terrell didn't answer. He was busy mowing down bad guys. "I'm gonna get that new PlayStation soon as it comes out."

"Oh, yeah? What bank are you gonna rob?" I asked.

Terrell glanced at the closed door to his room, then pulled a thick wad of bills out of his pocket and fanned them. Mostly fives and tens, and more money than I'd ever seen in one place.

"Where'd you get that?" I whispered.

"Smash n' grabs," he answered.

I gave him an uncertain look while he concentrated

7 **derisively:** abschätzig 11 **to mow down:** niedermähen
16 **wad:** Bündel 20 **smash and grab:** Überfall, bei dem gestohlen wird, was immer greifbar ist

on the game. Smashing car windows at red lights and grabbing chains off drivers' necks, or pocketbooks from seats, was a serious hustle. But it was hard to imagine how else he could have come up with that much gwap.

There was a knock on the door and Terrell quickly slid the money back into his pocket. "Who's there?"

The door opened and Laqueta looked in. Only, she was almost unrecognizable. Her skin was all ashy, her hair nappy, and she was wearing a long yellow T-shirt with stains on the front. It was hard to believe that she'd once been the prettiest girl in the projects. But that was before Darnell went out the window.

"Go get me a bottle of Cisco," she said.

"Go away," Terrell shot back, hunched over his game controller.

"Get me that bottle or I'll tell your momma how much money you got," Laqueta threatened.

Terrell narrowed his eyes at her. He didn't like people bossing him around in front of his friends.

"Come on," I said. "I want to get out of here anyway."

2 **pocketbook:** Handtasche 3 **a serious hustle:** ein ziemliches Ding 4 **gwap:** (ugs.) Kohle 13 **Cisco:** billiger Wein
14 **to hunch:** kauern, sich vorbeugen

Near the stairwell on the fourth floor we came across a bent old man gripping a walker with bony old hands. His hair was white, his yellow eyes bloodshot, and his skin hung from his face like baggy clothes.

"I need some food." When he spoke you saw more pink gum than teeth. Tied to the front of the walker was a basket with a few wrinkled dollar bills and some change inside.

"Give me the money," Terrell replied. "I'll get you food."

"Not you. Him." The old man pointed a shaky finger at me. "You Shanice's grandson, right? They say you a good boy. I ain't eat in two days. Get me some sardines and a loaf."

"Okay." I reached into the basket and took the money. "What apartment you in?"

"Don't matter," he said. "I'll wait for you here."

"You can't stand here and wait," I said. "Tell me what apartment you're in and I'll bring it to you."

The old man turned to Terrell. "You go away."

Terrell gave the old man a contemptuous look, then

2 **bent:** vornübergebeugt **walker:** Gehgestell, Rollator
6 **gum:** Zahnfleisch 14 **loaf [of bread]:** Brot
21 **contemptuous:** verächtlich

headed down the stairwell to the next floor. With his shaky wrinkled hand the old man grabbed my shirt sleeve and tugged me close so he could whisper in my ear. His breath smelled godawful. “Four G. But don’t go tellin’ that other boy. He’ll break in, steal everything I have.”

It was hard to imagine the old man had anything worth stealing, but I agreed just the same.

The closest food store was Wally’s. The front was boarded up and covered with colorful graffiti and tags. You wouldn’t have thought it was even a place of business unless you knew it was there. Inside the light was dim and a ceiling fan whirred. The sweet scent of rotten fruit hung in the air. Wally was a big fat walrus of a man who sat all day by the cash register. People said he kept a sawed-off shotgun under the counter.

“Don’t be comin’ in here to steal,” he warned when we entered. He had a green dishtowel draped around his fat neck, and his shirt was dark with sweat stains.

“You got sardines and a loaf?” I asked.

“Sardines over there.” Wally pointed a fat finger. “Bread over here. Get it quick. No hangin’ around.”

3 **to tug:** ziehen   14 **cash register:** Kasse

Terrell and I had hardly taken a step when Wally held out his hand at Terrell. "You buyin' something?"

My friend shook his head.

"Then wait outside," Wally said.

Terrell gave Wally his best narrow-eyed menacing hard hitta look, then went out. I got the food and paid for it. Back outside under the glaring yellow sun, Terrell muttered, "I'm gonna come back with my boys and bust that place up."

"You crazy?"

"You see the way he dissed me? Like I was gonna rob the place."

"He treated you like a gangbanger," I said. "I thought that's what you wanted."

In the heat we walked a block to the liquor store. The windows – covered with bars – were cracked and taped. Terrell pushed the buzzer beside the door and we looked up at the security camera so the owner could see our faces.

The door buzzed open. Inside was a narrow aisle with walls of thick scuffed Plexiglas rising to the ceiling on

6 **hitta:** (ugs. für "hitter") Schläger 8 **to bust sth. up:** etw. zerschlagen 11 **to diss s.o.:** jmd. abfertigen, respektlos behandeln 15 **liquor store:** Geschäft für alkoholische Getränke 21 **scuffed:** abgeschabt

both sides. Everything – the cash registers, counters, and shelves of bottles – was behind the Plexiglas.

"What do you boys want?" A tough-looking woman with red lips and a big head of dyed reddish-orange hair asked through some holes in the thick plastic.

"My cousin Laqueta wants some Cisco," Terrell said in his good-boy voice.

"Laqueta from where?" the woman asked suspiciously.

"Douglass."

Recognition softened the woman's expression. "The momma of that little boy who fell out the window last Christmas?"

Terrell nodded and slid some money through a slot. The woman opened a small door in the Plexiglas and pushed through a dark red bottle with a strawberry-colored label.

"Police ask where you got this bottle, what you gonna say?"

"Someone gave it to me," Terrell answered.

"Who?" the woman asked.

4 **dyed:** gefärbt

"I donno, some old man," Terrell answered.

The woman made a face. "Now why would some old man do that?"

"My momma gave it to us," I volunteered. "To bring to his momma."

The woman smiled and nodded. "That's right. That's what you say."

Back at Douglass, Terrell went to give the wine to Laqueta, and I brought the food to the old man in 4-G. He asked me if I wanted to come in, but I said no. I knew he was lonely. With the elevator broken he probably hadn't been downstairs in days, or maybe even weeks. I felt bad for him but I didn't want to enter his apartment.

When I got back to my apartment, Denzel was sitting in the living room with Nia.

"Let's bounce," he said when I came in.

"Where?" I glanced at Nia, who returned a tight, concerned look.

"Upstairs," Denzel said.

17 **to bounce:** (ugs.) sich verdrücken

Fourteen

On the fifteenth floor, Denzel stopped outside a door across the hall from the apartments I'd snuck into the previous winter. I could hear a TV inside. Denzel knocked three times, then paused and knocked twice.

I heard the clink of metal bolts and then Marcus opened the door. His broad, flat forehead glistened with sweat. Behind him were weights and a bench. Marcus gestured for me to come in and told Denzel he could go. Then he bolted the door shut. My heart was beating like mad and my breaths came short and fast.

"Thirsty?" Marcus asked.

I wasn't really, but I was afraid he'd be offended if I turned down his offer, so I nodded.

"Check the fridge. And get me a beer."

9 **to sneek in:** sich hineinschleichen 12 **bolt:** Riegel

The kitchen was clean and neat, the counter lined with bottles of vitamins and nutrition powders. The refrigerator was filled with malt liquor, wine, six-packs of soda, beer, and energy drinks. I got a beer for Marcus and a Coke for myself. Back in the living room Marcus was sitting on the weight bench doing curls with a barbell that looked like it must have weighed fifty pounds. The skin around his eyes was creased and his jaw was set. The veins in his forehead and right arm swelled as he lifted the weight over and over, until he let it fall to the floor with a thud. He sat there breathing hard for a few moments. Then he cracked the beer, took a gulp, and nodded at the weight. "Give it a try."

I grabbed the handle with both hands where he had used one. The first time I tried to lift it, I got it about an inch off the ground and then it pulled me back down. I tried again, pulling with all my might. I could feel my arms and body trembling under the strain, but I wasn't going to give up. I managed to get the barbell up to my knees and started to try to get it up to my waist. Marcus watched silently.

1 **neat:** ordentlich 2 **nutrition powders:** Nahrungsergänzungsmittel 3 **malt liquor:** Bier mit extrahohem Alkoholgehalt 4 **soda:** alkoholfreies Getränk mit Kohlensäure 6 **curl:** Armbeuge **barbell:** Hantel 11 **thud:** dumpfer Schlag 12 **gulp:** großer Schluck 17 **might:** Kraft, Stärke 18 **strain:** Anstrengung

"Okay," he finally said.

Thump! The barbell hit the floor harder than I'd wanted and I felt a little embarrassed. I sat down, clutching the cold soda can in my hands.

Marcus smiled. "You're supposed to drink it."

I did what I was told.

"When's those babies due?" Marcus asked.

"Two months, I think."

"Nia gonna go live with Denzel, or he gonna move in with you?"

The question caught me off guard. I'd heard no talk of either of those things happening. But it made sense that something like that might.

Marcus took another gulp. "How old are you?"

"Thirteen."

"Ever tell anyone about that window guard?"

"No."

"D'you think that had anything to do with Darnell?"

"Maybe." I couldn't believe it. Marcus obviously hadn't bothered to take a look at the window in Darnell's

11 **to catch s.o. off guard:** jmd. unvorbereitet treffen

room. But then, it was all guesswork. I couldn't prove anything.

Marcus studied me silently. "You got a lot of sense for your age, Kalon. More than a lot of dudes twice your age. Your momma was that way."

I looked up, surprised. "You knew her?"

"She used to babysit me and my brother and sister sometimes."

"You have a brother?"

"Had one."

"How –" I began and then caught myself. Even at the age of thirteen I knew he'd probably been shot, OD'd, or died from AIDS.

For a moment Marcus's eyes were soft and sad, and I wondered how many people had ever seen that look from him. Then he got up and took a white envelope from a pair of black pants hanging over the back of a chair. Sitting down on the exercise bench again, he held it open to me. Inside were bills. I thought I saw a hundred and a fifty. Marcus closed the envelope and sealed it with his tongue.

4 **dude:** Typ, Kerl 12 **to OD:** (kurz für "overdose") eine Überdosis nehmen 19 **bill:** Banknote

"Know what bail is, Kalon?" he asked.

I shook my head.

"Say I get arrested," Marcus said. "My trial may not get scheduled for six months. The police can keep me in jail till then unless I post bail." He handed me the envelope. "This is bail money. If I get arrested, I'll send word about what to do with it."

"You're gonna be arrested?" I asked.

Marcus chuckled. "Sooner or later. If I don't get killed first. You put that in a safe place. Don't tell anyone. Not even your gramma."

"Why me?"

"It can't come from anyone in the Disciples or the police'll know it's tainted. Gotta come from someone on the outside. Someone I can trust."

I looked down at the envelope, then thought of something and held it back toward him. "What if *you* tell someone? Word gets out I have this money, they'll kill me if I don't give it to them. Probably kill my sister and Gramma, too."

Marcus didn't take the envelope. "You keep it."

1 **bail:** Kaution 5 **to post bail:** eine Kaution stellen
14 **tainted:** belastet, nicht sauber

"Can't you find someone else?" I asked.

He shook his head slowly. "It's got to be you."

"Why?"

"'cause you're the only one that don't want it."

Fifteen

"Where'd you get that scrawny mutt, Lightbulb?" Bublz asked out in the yard a few days before school was set to start again. We were hanging around the bench. Felt like we'd spent the whole summer there.

"Found him," Lightbulb said. The little brown dog tugged at the clothes line leash. Its ribs showed through the fur and its paws looked too big for the rest of him.

"And how do you know he don't belong to someone else?" I asked.

"Anyone says he's theirs, I'll give him back." Lightbulb shrugged. "But so far no one's said nothin'."

Bublz shoved a handful of Cracker Jacks in his mouth and his cheeks bulged. "He's gonna choke himself if he keeps pullin' like that."

8 **scrawny:** klapprig **mutt:** Köter 13 **leash:** Leine
19 **Cracker Jacks:** eine Sorte karamellisiertes Popcorn
20 **to choke s.o.:** jmd. erdrosseln

"What's his name?"

"Snoop."

"Snoop Dog," Bublz smirked. "He's too dumb to know he's choking himself."

Lightbulb looked down at his new pet with concern. "He ain't dumb, is he, Kalon?"

"Naw, just young. He'll learn." I gazed around the yard. "Anyone wanna see Terrell?"

Bublz shook his head. "Too far to climb."

Lightbulb and I started toward the building. Snoop squirmed against the leash, sniffing everything. He got to an empty Twix wrapper and started to eat it.

"No, Snoop! You don't want that garbage." Lightbulb worked the candy wrapper out of Snoop's mouth.

"When was the last time you fed him?" I asked.

"Ain't fed him yet," Lightbulb answered.

"How long have you had him?"

"Since yesterday."

"And you haven't fed him at all? No wonder he's so hungry."

"Got nothin' to give him."

11 **to squirm:** sich winden

"After we see Terrell, we gotta get him something to eat," I said.

We went into the building and knocked on Terrell's door. It had been at least two days since I'd last seen him. We could hear the TV on loud inside.

The door opened and Terrell stood there bare-chested, wearing pajama bottoms.

Something was odd.

"Who's that?" Mrs. Blake came into view.

"Can Terrell come out?" Lightbulb asked.

"No, he can't," Mrs. Blake replied. "He's grounded. Can't see no friends, neither."

Lightbulb glanced at Terrell and dropped his voice. "You being punished?"

But he didn't drop his voice enough.

"Damn right he is," said Mrs. Blake. "One week in the house for stealin' money outa my purse."

Terrell's face colored, and he closed the door. Now I knew where his pocketful of money had come from. Damn liar.

Back outside, Lightbulb and I walked down Aber-

7 **pajama bottoms:** Schlafanzughose 11 **to be grounded:** Hausarrest haben

nathy. King Chicken was near Washington Carver Middle School. There was a parking lot in the front and extra spaces in the back, but hardly anyone ever went back there. A dented red dumpster leaned against a wall and the asphalt around it was littered with broken glass, paper cups and plates, straws and other garbage. The back lot smelled like rancid milk and garbage, but as soon as we got close to the dumpster, Snoop started yelping and pawing at the ground, tugging as hard as he could.

"Whoa, Snoop, we'll get there!" Lightbulb gasped as the little dog strained against the leash with all of its might.

I found a gray milk crate to stand on and managed to reach in, grab some white paper bags, and toss them onto the ground. Snoop tore into them and started jawing on a piece of chicken.

"Guess you were right," Lightbulb said.

The squeal of tires made us jump. A black Land Rover with dark windows and big glittering rims screeched around the side of the building and skidded to a stop.

4 **dumpster:** Müllcontainer 9 **to yelp:** aufheulen, jaulen **to paw:** mit den Pfoten scharren 16 **to jaw:** (ugs. für "chew") kauen 19 **squeal:** Quietschen 20 **to screech:** kreischen 21 **to skid:** rutschen, schleudern

Lightbulb and I ducked behind the dumpster. Snoop stayed out in the open, chewing on his chicken.

Three men got out of the Land Rover. From the green and yellow beads around their necks and the green bandanas in their pockets, I knew that they were Gentry Gangstas. I put my hand on Lightbulb's shoulder and slowly drew him back into the shadows behind the dumpster to make sure we wouldn't be seen.

One of the Gangstas was medium height, with broad shoulders, and wore a baseball cap backward. Reaching into the car, he yanked out a skinny old crusty-looking man with a scruffy gray beard and dirty, torn ghetto clothes. He looked like an old hype or wino.

The Gangsta with the baseball cap pushed the old guy down on his knees before the other two men. One was narrowly built with very dark skin, sharp chiseled features, and long pointed sideburns. He stood with his arms crossed and an impassive expression on his face. Like a judge. The other was just plain big, with a shaved head. He grabbed the old scruffy guy by the collar and shook him like a floppy doll.

4 **beads:** Perlen(ketten) 11 **to yank:** zerren, reißen
12 **scruffy:** struppig, ungepflegt 13 **hype:** (ugs.) Junkie, Drogenabhängiger 16 **chiseled:** gemeißelt 17 **pointed:** spitz zulaufend **sideburns:** Koteletten 18 **impassive:** ungerührt
21 **floppy doll:** Schlenkerpuppe

"This is your last chance," he threatened. "Tell him!"

"I don't know nothin'!" the old man trembled with fear.

The giant nodded at the Gangsta with the baseball cap, who pulled out a big black gun and stuck it against the old guy's neck. My hand was still on Lightbulb's shoulder and I felt him shudder and tense at the sight of the gun. He started to breathe hard and fast.

The gunholder's voice was cold as ice. "We don't want to kill you, man," he said. "But if we have to we will."

"But I swear," the old guy stammered. "I didn't see nothin'. I didn't hear nothin'. I don't know nothin'. I swear it, Mr. Rance."

I caught my breath. There was only one Rance, and he was the leader of the Gentry Gangstas. And that meant the big Gangsta was Big D, the second in command.

A dozen feet from them, Snoop began to retch and gag. Rance and the other gangbangers glanced at him and then back to the old guy.

"This is your last chance," Rance said.

18 **retch:** krächzend würgen **gag:** würgen, nach Luft schnappen

"But I don't know!" the old man wailed. "I swear!"

Crack! The Gangsta with the gun grabbed him by the hair and smashed the butt of his weapon hard against his nose. The old guy clutched his face with his hands and bright red blood began to seep out between his gnarled fingers. Lightbulb tensed even more. He was breathing so hard I was afraid he might pass out.

Snoop kept retching and shaking his head as if something was caught in his throat. The gangbangers looked at him again, then Rance kneeled down until he was eye-level with the bleeding man and began to speak in a calm voice. "Now, listen, Rodney, you really think this is worth dying for?"

Snoop howled and gagged more loudly. At the interruption, Rance turned his head sharply with an annoyed expression. As if taking a cue, the Gangsta with the baseball cap aimed his gun at the little dog.

"Don't!" Lightbulb screamed. Before I could stop him, he jumped out from behind the dumpster.

Startled, Big D quickly pulled his gun and aimed it at my friend as he kneeled beside the choking dog. Afraid

1 **to wail:** heulen 3 **butt:** Griff 5 **gnarled:** knorrig, verwachsen
7 **to pass out:** ohnmächtig werden 14 **to howl:** jaulen
15 **annoyed:** ärgerlich, angenervt 16 **cue:** Stichwort

that they might shoot both Lightbulb and Snoop, I stepped out from behind the dumpster.

"What the hell!" Rance grumbled.

My heart was racing and I felt my lungs expanding and contracting as if I'd just sprinted a quarter mile. Two weapons were now aimed directly at me. That was the end. The merest movement of a finger would send pieces of lead ripping through my flesh.

Slowly raising my hands to shoulder height, my eyes met Rance's.

"Anyone else behind there?" Rance asked, almost amused.

I tried to sound calm. "No, sir. Please don't aim those guns at us. We ain't done nothing."

But the guns stayed on Lightbulb and me, as if the gangbangers knew from experience that this was what their leader expected.

"What're you kids doin' back here?" Rance asked.

"J...Just gettin' my dog some food," Lightbulb said, hugging Snoop and trembling from head to toe. "Please don't hurt us, please."

7 **merest:** kleinste

Rance's eyes returned to mine. I stared at the black tear tattoos beside his eyes. Snoop wretched loudly and coughed up some chewed chicken and bones. The little dog began to whimper.

"Get out of here," Rance said.

Lightbulb picked up Snoop and we ran.

4 **to whimper:** wimmern

Sixteen

It was the evening before school was supposed to start. Terrell's punishment for stealing was over and he and I were in his room playing video Grand Theft Auto on his X-Box.

"Terrell!" Mrs. Blake hollered urgently. We raced out into the living room. Laqueta was flat on her back on the floor with her eyes rolled up into her head and only the whites showing. Terrell's momma was straddling her, slapping her face, and crying "Come on, baby, wake up! Wake up!" When she saw us she yelled, "Call 911! Then go downstairs and wait for the ambulance guys and bring them up here."

By the time Terrell and I got to the yard, we could hear the sirens. A few moments later a boxy red and white

15 **to straddle:** quer auf jmd. sitzen   17 **911:** Notrufnummer
21 **boxy:** kastenförmig

ambulance pulled up to the curb with the lights flashing. The two men inside took their time getting out. One was white, the other black. They looked around with wary, unhappy expressions like this was the last place in the world they wanted to be.

"Come on," Terrell said anxiously, pointing back at the building. "My cousin's out cold. We don't know if she's passed out and OD'd or what."

"She drink? Take drugs?" asked the black man.

"Both," said Terrell.

"Better get the stretcher," the white one said and they went around and opened the back doors, still taking their sweet time. The black ambulance man started to wheel the stretcher toward the building while his colleague stayed behind with the truck.

"Maybe you both better come," I said to him. "Could take two to carry her down."

"Or maybe you got friends in there waiting to mug us," he returned. "Or we'll get back here and the ambulance'll be ransacked for drugs and needles. I stay here and keep an eye on the truck."

7 **out cold:** bewusstlos 18 **to mug:** überfallen
20 **to ransack:** plündern

It was no use arguing. Terrell and I followed the black ambulance man as he wheeled the stretcher toward the building. He kept looking around as if he expected at any second to be jumped. He pushed the stretcher toward the elevator.

"The elevator's broke," Terrell said, and pointed at the stairwell. "We gotta take the stairs."

The ambulance man hesitated. "How far?"

"Sixth floor," said Terrell.

The man shook his head. "You'll have to bring her down."

"You crazy!?" Terrell began to bluster, but I grabbed his arm to stop him and asked, "How?"

"Make a sling with a blanket," he said. "Four of you can do it if each one holds a corner. Won't take long."

By the time we got to the apartment, Denzel and Marcus were there. They'd moved Laqueta to the couch, but she was still limp. More foamy spit dripped from the corner of her mouth.

"Where's the ambulance men?" Marcus asked.

"Wouldn't climb up the stairs," I said.

4 **to be jumped:** angefallen werden 14 **sling:** Trage
18 **foamy:** schaumig

Marcus cursed and told Mrs. Blake to find a blanket. Laqueta's arms and legs flopped every which way and her head rolled loosely. Marcus, Denzel, Terrell and I each picked up a corner. With the four of us lifting her, she felt lighter than I'd expected.

We started down the stairs. Marcus and Denzel went first because they were taller and stronger. Even then Terrell and I struggled to hold up our end.

We were on the fourth floor when the shooting started outside. The sound of people shouting drifted up the stairs.

"What the hell?" Marcus grunted. He momentarily lowered the blanket with Laqueta to the floor, then lifted again. "We gotta get her down. Come on."

The lobby was full of people who'd run inside to get away from the shooting. Most stayed clear of the doors and were huddled near the stairs. We put Laqueta down on the lobby floor and once again Mrs. Blake hysterically slapped her face, trying to wake her. Meanwhile I scanned the crowd, but didn't see the ambulance man. Snoop trotted by, sniffing here and there. That meant

17 **to huddle:** sich zusammenkauern

Lightbulb was around. I found him hiding under the stairs with his eyes squeezed tight and his fingers stuck in his ears.

"You seen an ambulance man?" I asked, but he didn't seem to hear me. "Lightbulb!" I shook his shoulder.

"Huh?"

"Was there an ambulance man here?"

"He left," Lightbulb stammered. "The second the shooting started."

Jamar came in from outside with a Disciple named Tyrone, who was holding his arm. People said Tyrone was the skinniest man they'd ever seen. It was almost hard to believe a bullet could find anything to hit, but you could see bright red blood seeping around his fingers, darkening his shirt, and dripping to the floor. Marcus spoke to them, then jerked his head at Denzel and Jamar to go out into the dark with him.

"Come on," Terrell whispered. Outside the night air smelled of burnt gunpowder. Terrell and I pressed ourselves against the building. The bricks still felt warm from being in the sun all day. In the dark the yard looked

20 **brick:** Ziegel

empty, but slowly I began to see shapes. A woman was cradling a baby behind a tree near an overturned baby stroller. Two old men lay on the ground under a bench, covering their heads with their arms.

Pop! Pop! Pop!

Terrell and I hit the ground. The shots had come from around the corner of the building. Terrell crawled on his hands and knees to the corner and peeked. The shooting stopped and he waved for me to join him. I scampered up. Marcus had ducked behind a bench. Denzel crouched behind a metal garbage can.

Pop! Pop! Pop!

They both fired and then moved forward as if to force the invaders back Abernathy Avenue. Jamar followed, reaching each spot only after Marcus or Denzel left it.

More shots, then car doors slammed and car tires screeched loudly. There was silence for a moment. Then the normal sounds of a summer evening – car horns, the rumble of bus engines, music, even voices – slowly began to return.

Terrell and I stayed behind the corner of the building.

9 **to scamper:** hastig laufen 14 **invader:** Eindringling

Out in the yard, Jamar rose slowly to his feet. But where were Marcus and Denzel?

People began to come out of their hidings slowly and carefully, stopping and listening before taking another step.

There was still no sign of Marcus or Denzel. Suddenly I felt scared. Marcus wasn't just the leader of the Disciples. In a way he was the stern father none of us boys had. He gave us jobs, issued orders, settled disputes, and kept people in line. It wasn't until that moment that I realized how people depended on him and needed to know he was there.

Two figures came around the corner. Even in the dark I could see that their clothes were disheveled and their arms hung loose at their sides as if they were exhausted from the terror and effort. As Marcus passed, he glared at Jamar and spit on the ground. Jamar began to say something, then caught himself and clammed up. Terrell and I stepped out from behind the corner of the building and followed them into the lobby. By now most of the people had left. But a few women were bent over La-

3 **hiding:** Versteck 9 **to issue orders:** Befehle erteilen **to settle a dispute:** einen Streit schlichten 14 **disheveled:** unordentlich 18 **to clam up:** verstummen

queta. Someone had rolled up a shawl under her head, and someone else was fanning her with a newspaper while Mrs. Blake dabbed the wet cloth on her niece's forehead.

"Kalon!" My sister's anxious voice called from the stairwell. "Anyone seen Kalon?"

"In the lobby," I yelled back.

Nia came to the top of the stairs with her hands on her big belly and consternation on her face. "What're you doin' down here?"

"Helping," I said.

"Gramma wants you upstairs *right now!*"

I could feel people's eyes on me. She came down the stairs, grabbed me by the arm and squeezed hard, and suddenly I knew it wasn't just Gramma who wanted me out of harm's way.

Meanwhile, Marcus bent down and lifted Laqueta in his arms. Her head rolled back. "We'll take my car."

Someone held the door open and Marcus went through sideways. Denzel, Mrs. Blake, and Terrell followed. Jamar was nowhere to be seen. Everyone left in

2 **to fan s.o.:** jmd. Luft zufächern 9 **consternation:** Ärger, Missfallen

the lobby watched silently. Marcus was a gang leader and drug dealer, almost surely a murderer, and as brutal and hard as anyone I'd ever met. And he was the only hero I knew.

Seventeen

After school on Friday I walked home feeling like there was a big black cloud over my head. Tanisha still thought we were going to the movies that night with LaChandra and Michael, but I had no money and no way to get any. I couldn't decide which was worse: telling Tanisha we couldn't go, or going and letting her pay.

"Hey," someone said.

I looked up.

Marcus's black Mercedes was rolling slowly along the curb beside me. He steered with one hand and leaned his elbow out the open window. "What's wrong?"

"Who said anything's wrong?" I replied.

"Looks like something's got you down," he said, pulling the car to the curb. "I been driving alongside you for almost a whole block and you ain't looked up once. You got a problem, maybe I can help."

That reminded me of something. "Laqueta okay?"

"Yeah, she's back home now." He gazed at me with those searching eyes. "You gonna tell me what's botherin' you?"

"I can take care of it," I said.

If a muscle in Marcus's face moved, I didn't see it. He just looked at me long and steady. "What grade you in at school?"

"Seventh."

"How you doing?"

"Okay. Mr. Brand says maybe I could go to the Hewlett School over in Beech Hill."

"Beech Hill's pretty far," Marcus said. "You gotta take some kind of a test to get in?"

"Yeah. Vocabulary, math, a lot of stuff."

Marcus rubbed his chin. "So how come you're moping along like your dog just got run over?" he asked.

Suddenly I knew I was going to tell him. It was the kind of thing you wanted to talk about with a guy with

18 **to mope:** Trübsal blasen

experience. "I'm supposed to go on a date tonight and I don't have any money."

Marcus nodded slowly. "That's messed up. How bad do you want to go?"

"That's just it," I said. "I don't care if I go or not. But my girl wants to go so bad she says she'll pay."

"No way." Marcus shook his head, and I knew he understood. His arm disappeared from the open window. When it reappeared, a bill was folded between his dark fingers. "Fifty do you?"

I hesitated. "What you want in return?"

"Nothing."

That night Tanisha and I went to the movies with LaChandra and Michael. It was the first time I'd ever been alone in the dark with Tanisha – the first time I'd ever been alone in the dark with any girl – and it meant the world to me.

After the movie I went straight home. The streets were crowded and noisy, but I felt like I was somewhere else.

Without Tanisha I was more aware of the night around me. The scent of barbeque was in the air even though summer was pretty much over. The subwoofers booming from the slow-moving rides cruising the streets, the girls and guys flirting, the styled-up folks waiting in lines to get into clubs. It was Friday night and everyone was trying to get what they'd waited all week for.

I got back to Douglass. Out in the yard people were having a homecoming party for Derek who'd just gotten out of prison. There was barbeque and dancing to loud music from a sound system rigged up to a car battery. People were drinking and laughing. Jamar was talking with a girl with a big chest and short brown hair pasted tight to her skull. In the shadows near one of the trees, Denzel was dancing closely with a skanky-looking girl in high heels with bleached blond pigtails and a short, low-cut dress. All I could do was pretend not to see him and hope nobody told Nia.

I was about to go in when I noticed someone on the bench, bent forward with his head on his arms. "Terrell?"

2 **scent:** Duft 3 **subwoofers:** Basslautsprecher
4 **to cruise:** spazieren fahren 11 **to rig up to:** an etw. anschließen 13 **to paste:** ankleben 15 **skanky:** (ugs.) billig, wie eine Schlampe

My best friend lifted his head. Even in the dark I could see that one of his eyes was swollen shut, and dried blood caked his nose and lips.

"What the hell?" I said.

He made a fist. On the back of his hand were three ugly reddish cigarette burns. Then he pulled a string of black and white beads from under his shirt and gave me the sign of the Disciples. A crooked smile worked its way onto his swollen lips. He was in.

3 **to cake:** verkleben

FOURTEEN YEARS OLD

When President Bush signed the No Child Left Behind Act in January of 2002, he promised that by 2014 the quality of inner-city school education would catch up to that in suburban schools. But by 2007 the gap between black and white eighth graders was worse than ever.

Eighteen

"I wish we could be alone," Tanisha whispered in my ear. We were at Tanisha's locker between classes. She had her back to the wall and I pressed against her.

"Me, too," I whispered and kissed her. She smelled like cocoa butter, and the mixed sensations of pleasure and yearning were enough to make my knees feel weak. But it was nearly impossible for us to be alone. Lately there'd been more and more shooting between the Disciples and the Gangstas. Anyone from Douglass found in Gentry territory was liable to be shot. Her hair smelled so clean and her perfume was sweet and when we were close like that it felt like nothing else mattered.

"Maybe you could come over after school," she whispered with closed eyes as I kissed her neck.

9 **locker:** Spind, Schließfach 17 **to be liable to be shot:** gute Chancen haben, erschossen zu werden

"I don't know," I whispered back. "I mean, I want to ..."

"My momma'll be at work and William is hardly ever around." Odd as it may sound, I had never met Tanisha's brother William. I only knew that he was a Gentry Gangsta.

"Let me think about it ..." We pressed together, feeling more heat than the friction of our clothes alone could create.

"Enough of that, you two," Ms. Rodriguez snapped sharply.

I backed slowly away from Tanisha. The days of jumping when a teacher gave an order had passed.

"I'm getting tired of telling you two to find someplace else for that." The white-haired assistant principal focused her eyes on me. "Kalon, come with me. We need to talk."

We went down the hall to her office where she pointed to a wooden chair. "Have a seat."

The office was cold and she pulled a pink sweater over her shoulders.

8 **friction:** Aneinanderreiben

She searched through a pile of folders on her desk. "Mr. Brand left instructions for you to take the entrance exam for the Hewlett School." She stared over the top of the folder at me with a questioning look.

"What happened to him, anyway?" I asked. It was November and I had not yet seen him around school.

"He took a job in the suburbs. It's a pity. He was an excellent teacher. We would have welcomed him back."

I gazed through the dirt-streaked window covered by bars. Out on the sidewalk a crusty old bum who looked like he was wearing three coats lugged a huge clear plastic bag filled with empty cans and bottles.

"Now, you understand, Kalon, that we're only allowed to submit a certain number of students for that exam. Have you prepared?"

I shook my head.

"Let's take a look at your transcript." She turned to her computer. "Hmm, well, you are certainly one of the better students, especially among the boys."

"Mr. Brand said I was reading at grade level," I said proudly.

10 **bum:** (ugs.) Penner 11 **to lug:** schleppen
14 **to submit:** anmelden, einreichen
17 **transcript:** hier: Notenübersicht

"Let's see the standardized test results." She typed and a different screen appeared on the computer. Her eyebrows dipped and the corners of her mouth turned down. "City-wide, your test scores are in the twenty-third percentile."

"What's that mean?" I asked, although I could tell by her expression that it wasn't good.

"Compared to students from all the other schools, you're in the bottom quarter."

The radiator made a faint gurgling sound, as if water was struggling to get through.

"It's not your fault, Kalon," Ms. Rodriguez said tapping the tip of a bony finger against her lower lip. "Many children get private tutoring or special preparation. Things we can't give students here."

Secretly, I felt relief. I didn't want to leave Tanisha and take a bus every day back and forth to Beech Hill. And now I didn't have to feel bad about letting Mr. Brand down because he could have come back to Washington Carver this year if he'd really cared.

Ms. Rodriguez tapped the bottom of the folder

1 **standardized test results:** Ergebnisse von Zentralprüfungen
4 **scores:** Ergebnisse **percentile:** Prozent-Anteil
14 **private tutoring:** Privatunterricht, Nachhilfe

against the desk. “All right?” She had other things to do. It was time for me to go. I got up and started to leave.

“Kalon?” she said. “One other thing. Your friend Raydale Diggs.”

“Who?”

“I believe you call him Lightbulb?”

It had been so long since I heard his real name that I’d forgotten.

“Maybe you could do us a favor,” Ms. Rodriguez continued. “He’s one of the brightest children we’ve ever seen here and we would like him to apply to the Hewlett School, but he seems reluctant. Perhaps you’d talk to him? You’re a friend so he might listen to you.”

13 **reluctant:** zögernd, zurückhaltend

Nineteen

Nia had twins – a boy named Xavier and a girl named Jayda – and the population in our apartment increased by three, not two, because Denzel moved in. Gramma gave her room to the new family. Now she slept on the couch and I slept on the floor on a small mattress that we hid behind the curtains during the day.

Xavier and Jayda cried a lot. Sometimes they cried all day and half the night. It seemed like those babies had taken over the whole apartment. The kitchen counter was covered with plastic baby bottles and cans of baby formula, and the garbage can was a heap of stinky pampers. Hand-washed baby clothes and maternity bras hung in the bathroom.

I spent as much time as I could outside.

17 **baby formula:** Milchpulver, Fläschchennahrung

Terrell and I were hanging around the bench talking to Precious and listening to Coolio on Terrell's boombox. Precious had put on a lot of eye make-up. Her tight white tee shirt said, "So Many Boyz, So Little Time." The material was so thin that you could see the pink bra underneath.

"Hey, your daddy see you dress like that?" Terrell asked.

Precious's face hardened. "He ain't around no more." She glanced at the boom box balanced on Terrell's knees. "Why you got that hunk of junk? Can't you afford an iPod or an iPhone?"

"What's the point?" Terrell asked, slightly annoyed.

"Get a lot more songs than those cheap bootleg CDs you play." Precious spoke in a taunting, angry way, as if challenging your manhood. So different from that cute little girl a few years back in the new pink jacket who was so proud of the Christmas presents her daddy got for her.

Terrell played it slow and cool, like he had nothing to prove to her. "Trouble with that iPod is you can't listen

11 **hunk of junk:** fette Schrottkiste 16 **to challenge:** herausfordern, infrage stellen

with your peeps," he said, gesturing toward me. He put on his seducer's smile. "Hey, bunny, you want to go out sometime?"

"With who?" Precious asked and turned her mascared eyes as if looking for someone worthy of her.

"Who do you think?" Terrell asked.

Precious gave him a cool appraisal. "You? You ain't nothing but a two bit crack dealer. Where we gonna go? You got money? You got a car? You even old enough to drive? 'cause I ain't goin' on no bus date."

"I can get a car if I want," Terrell said.

"Uh huh. Sure you can," Precious said doubtfully.

A woman came up, all ashy skin and bones and missing teeth and filthy, ragged clothes. The walking dead. She handed Terrell some money and he pointed at a shorty leaning against a wall, head bent, thumbs flying over the controls of a PSP2. The kid couldn't have been more than nine years old. The woman went over and he led her inside the building.

Dealers used shorties to hold their crack and weed and pills because the worst thing the cops could do was

2 **seducer:** Verführer 7 **appraisal:** Beurteilung, Bewertung
8 **two bit:** klein, mickrig 17 **PSP2:** PlayStation 2

confiscate the drugs and take the kid home to his momma. Everyone knew the courts wouldn't put eight and nine year olds in juvie. The mothers knew it, too. Some of them waited until the cops left and then sent their kids back to work.

"So maybe you got some money," Precious conceded, but what she didn't know was that almost every penny went to the Disciples, not Terrell. She took a compact out of her bag and checked her make-up.

"Ahem." Terrell cleared his throat. "So? You wanna go out?"

Precious gazed up over the compact at him. "You better have a car, and you better take me someplace nice." She snapped the compact shut, spun on her toes and walked away.

Terrell grinned and held out his palm for me to slap. "Friday night's startin' to look real good."

The day drifted past. I hung around the bench because it was better than being inside listening to those babies cry. Girls played jump rope. Old folks hobbled past on canes

1 **to confiscate:** beschlagnahmen 3 **juvie:** (kurz für "juvenile detention") Jugendknast 6 **to concede:** einräumen
8 **compact:** Puderdose mit Spiegel im Klappdeckel
21 **to hobble:** humpeln **cane:** Stock

or behind walkers. Terrell and the shortie didn't sell anything more so Terrell sent him home.

Bublz joined us. "Look what I got," he said and fanned out a bunch of King Chicken coupons. "Buy one, get one free."

I was hungry. Most of the food stamps and welfare money that month had gone toward baby formula and supplies.

Terrell hadn't left the bench in hours. He had to be hungry, too. "Can't," said Terrell.

Bublz looked around. "Come on. You'll be back in twenty minutes. No one'll know you was gone."

On our way to King Chicken we met Lightbulb, pulled by Snoop, who'd grown to be a medium-size dog, but was still as wild as a pup.

"You gotta train that dog, Lightbulb," Terrell said.

"He's trained," Lightbulb insisted.

"Hey," I said trying to change the topic, "Ms. Rodriguez wants to know why you won't try for that Hewlett School."

"My momma can't pay for no bus," Lightbulb said.

8 **supplies:** Vorräte, Zubehör 15 **pup:** Welpe

"Ms. Rodriguez says he's one of the smartest they've ever seen."

"Lightbulb?" Terrell smirked. "Sure, he's got glasses."

I suggested that Terrell and Bulbz go ahead so I could talk with Lightbulb.

"It ain't about the bus fare," I said when we were out of Terrell's earshot.

Lightbulb scuffed his foot against the ground. "I don't want to go, Kalon. Just want to stay where I am."

"But this is nowhere."

"I'm happy here."

"For now. But then what? You gonna be a gangbanger?"

Lightbulb shook his head. "No. What are *you* gonna do?"

I didn't answer because I didn't know. By now we'd reached the corner of Abernathy and Beacon. We stood there and watched all those cars pass. All those people with places to go. Even Snoop got quiet. It felt like we were standing on the edge of the world. In front of us

7 **to be about:** um etwas gehen

was the broad six lanes of traffic racing past day and night. To the east was the boundary line with Gentry. To the north was the razor-wire fence to keep us out of the rail yard, and to the west was the Flats.

Sometimes it felt like we were on an island in the middle of everything, but unable, or unwilling, to get off.

After a while Snoop started to pull on the leash again. He wanted to go back to Douglass. As if even he felt safer there.

A few minutes later we were in a booth, working through a bucket of legs and breasts and slurping from big cups of soda.

"I'm takin' out Precious Friday night," Terrell announced.

"I thought she only dates older guys," said Bublz.

Terrell grinned. "Older guys ... and me."

"She said you had to drive," I reminded him.

"I can get a car," Terrell replied as if it was as easy as buying a candy bar. "Jamar taught me how."

12 **booth:** hier: Sitzecke in einem Fast-Food-Restaurant
13 **bucket of legs and breasts:** Familienportion frittiertes Hühnchen

"Just because you learned how to steal one doesn't mean you know how to drive one," I said.

"How hard could it be?" Terrell waved at the traffic outside. "Look at those dumbasses drivin' around."

The door to King Chicken swung open and Marcus marched in. Terrell and Bublz had their backs to the door and didn't notice him. But I did. Terrell must've seen it in my face because he started to turn around.

Wham! Marcus smacked him so hard it knocked our cups over, spilling soda all over the table and our clothes. A lady with two small kids in the next booth screamed. Bublz cowered in the corner of the booth, his eyes squeezed shut and his arms covering his head. I jumped up, my lap dark with spilled soda. Terrell was too stunned by the blow to move.

Wham! Marcus smacked him again, so hard it felt like a bomb going off. Everyone in the King Chicken stopped eating. Some started to leave.

Marcus raised his open hand again. "I say you could leave that bench?" Marcus demanded.

"Wasn't nothin' happening," Terrell stammered and

9 **to smack:** ohrfeigen 12 **to cower:** sich ducken, zusammenkauern
14 **stunned:** benommen, betäubt

huddled against Bublz, who was still cowering in a corner.

Marcus grabbed him by the collar and yanked him up with one hand until they were practically nose to nose. "You don't decide that, understand? You don't decide nothin'. You just do what I tell you."

"I'm tellin' you," Terrell said in a quavering voice. "Wasn't no one buyin' nothin'."

Marcus flinched and glanced around. He let go of Terrell's collar, then grabbed him by the hair and yanked him out of the booth.

"Ow! Ow! Man, stop it!" Terrell wailed. "I'll go!"

But Marcus didn't let go. He dragged Terrell out to the parking lot. I followed, keeping my distance. Behind me, Bublz took off down the sidewalk as fast as he could. Still holding Terrell by the hair, Marcus pressed him against the wall. Terrell stared at the ground, unwilling to look the gang leader in the eye.

"Mistake number one," Marcus growled in a low, ominous voice. "You don't leave that bench unless I tell you to. Ever. Understand?"

3 **collar:** Kragen 20 **ominous:** drohend

"I understand," he sniffed.

"Mistake number two," Marcus continued. "You don't talk business when anyone else can hear. Understand?"

Terrell nodded, blinking rapidly. Tears ran down his cheeks and hit the ground near his feet. He started to wheeze and quickly dug out his inhaler. Marcus watched him gasp for breath. He stared at the dark spots on the ground. Letting go of Terrell's hair, he held his hand close to Terrell's face. My friend winced as if expecting another blow. But instead, Marcus patted his cheek.

"Hey," he said gently. "Everybody makes a mistake."

Terrell looked up at him with reddened eyes, and sniffed. "It ain't fair. I sit all day on that bench. Most days I don't even sell fifty dollars' worth of rock. Then I got to give it all to you. I'd make more workin' here." He nodded at the King Chicken.

"I told you it takes time," Marcus said. "You gotta work your way up. Pay your dues. Two, three years from now you'll be makin' more in a day than you could make at this place in a month."

7 **to dig out:** herauskramen 15 **rock:** Crack
19 **to pay one's dues:** Lehrgeld bezahlen

Terrell nodded, and wiped his eyes with the back of his hand. Marcus looked at me. "Both of you in the car."

Being a Disciple, Terrell rode in the front while I sat in the back. Back at Douglass, Marcus parked on Abernathy and turned to Terrell. "Do your job. And don't let me ever see you leave that bench again."

Terrell got out. I slid across the back seat to get out, too, but Marcus looked over the seat at me. "How's them little babies doin'?"

"Okay."

"Denzel move in?"

I nodded.

"Must be getting kind of crowded in there."

"Uh huh."

"Ever think that someday you could have a place of your own?" he said. "A place to bring that cute girlfriend of yours."

I glanced out the window at Terrell, who'd gotten back up on the bench.

"That won't be you," Marcus said. "Still got that envelope I gave you?"

"Uh huh."

"Ever tell anyone?"

I shook my head.

"See, Kalon, the Disciples is like a company," Marcus said. "Different guys get different jobs. All depends on what the boss thinks you're good for. Right now Terrell's on that bench because that's what he's good for. You'd be good for other things. Things that pay a lot better."

I gazed at his tear tattoo. Maybe I should have been afraid, but I wasn't. I'd noticed something about Marcus. He could get real mad when you did something wrong, but he also listened when you spoke your mind. "I think you forgot to tell Terrell that there's a chance in two, three years he'll be makin' good money. But there's a better chance that he'll be dead or in jail."

"He knows that," Marcus conceded. "He'd have to be stupid not to."

It got quiet in the car.

"Listen, Kalon," he said. "You're a smart kid. Not school smart, street smart. It ain't something they give grades for. It's just something you're born with."

12 **to speak one's mind:** seine Meinung sagen

"Something I got from my momma?"

"That's right."

"If she was so smart, how come she's dead?"

Marcus gazed at me thoughtfully. "Bad luck. She was in the wrong place at the wrong time. Could have been anyone."

"Not me," I said.

"Even you."

Marcus's face hardened. I turned and saw that a police car was behind us. It was Officer Patterson. Marcus tilted his head toward the door. I got out and he drove away, but Officer Patterson didn't. He just sat in his car, watching me.

4 **bad luck:** Pech

Twenty

Rain swept down in sheets. Tanisha and I pulled our hoodies up and jogged quickly along the sidewalk, sometimes ducking in doorways when the downpour got too hard.

We were in Gentry. The buildings weren't high like Douglass. They were newer and mostly four stories, set in circles with walkways like spokes meeting in a central courtyard. On the outside they might have looked nicer, but in the lobby of Tanisha's building the mailboxes lining the wall were smashed just like the ones in my building. Tanisha pulled back her dripping hood and shook out her hair. Her eyes beamed. I wanted to pull off my wet hood, too, but I didn't dare.

Tanisha's apartment was dark and quiet. The kitchen

8 **in sheets:** in Strömen 10 **downpour:** Wolkenbruch
14 **spoke:** Speiche

was neat, the counter clear and the sink empty. The couch in the living room was covered with clear plastic, not a sheet and blanket. Tanisha led me down the hall and into her room. A big poster of Will Smith hung on the wall along with lots of sketches of women in dresses and skirts. Tanisha wanted to be a fashion designer, and there were sketch pads on the floor beside neat piles of fashion magazines.

Tanisha sat on the bed and pulled me down next to her. She leaned her head on my shoulder. For a while we just sat there catching our breaths after running, our legs hanging over the edge of the bed. The idea that I was in Gentry territory, in the home of an actual Gentry Gangsta, was stuck in my head, making it hard to relax.

Tanisha pulled off her hoody. "You wanna keep that hoody on?" she asked, teasing.

"Oh, yeah." I took it off and let it fall to the floor. Tanisha kissed my neck and then my ear, but I was still tense.

She backed off. "What's wrong?"

"I'm sorry, Tani. It's just bein' here."

7 **sketch pad:** Skizzenblock 19 **tense:** angespannt

"My momma won't be home for at least an hour and a half."

"And William?"

"I *told* you. He's never home." She leaned close and began to kiss my neck and ears again. I wanted to stop worrying and turned my face toward hers and we began to kiss.

Bang! A door closed somewhere in the apartment. I sat up straight and exchanged a wide-eyed look with Tanisha.

"It must be him!" she gasped.

My heart began to hammer. I was trapped. The window had bars across it. The bed? No, you never hid under a bed. If you were found there, you were defenseless. I got up and stood by the closet, ready to disappear inside.

From out in the hall came the sound of the refrigerator door opening and closing. The TV went on.

"Doesn't sound like he's leavin'," I whispered.

Tanisha bit her lip and looked at the clock on her night table.

12 **trapped:** in der Falle 14 **defenseless:** wehrlos
15 **closet:** Kleiderschrank

"You gotta sneak out," Tanisha said. "I'll unlock the front door, then go talk to William. You wait here. When I ask him if it's supposed to keep raining, that means the coast is clear. You tip toe down the hall and let yourself out. Okay?"

I don't know why we smiled at each other, but we did. Tanisha kissed me quick on the lips and left the room. I pulled my damp hoody back on and stood in the doorway, listening. But the TV was loud and it was hard to tell whether I was hearing Tanisha and William, or the people on the TV.

I stepped quietly into the hall. The living room was on the left and I stopped just before it and listened. Now all I heard was the TV. Then Tanisha said loudly, "So is it gonna keep raining or not?"

"What are you hollerin' for?" an annoyed male voice asked. "And why're you askin' me that when you just asked me a minute ago? What're you lookin' at anyway?"

"Nothing!" Tanisha answered with a frightened gasp.

1 **to sneak out:** sich hinausschleichen
4 **the coast is clear:** die Luft ist rein

I heard shifting sounds and plastic squeak as if someone had just risen from the couch.

"You don't have to get up!" Tanisha protested.

Her brother's answer came in footsteps. Out in the hall I considered dashing back to Tanisha's room, but there wasn't time. Instead I raised my hands to shoulder height so that William would see that I was unarmed. He stepped out into the hall and started when he saw me. I didn't dare looking at his face. I was too busy watching his hand reach toward his belt.

Tanisha rushed into the hall behind him. "William! Don't! He's my friend!"

William pulled a black gun from his waist and pointed it at me. My heart beat harder and I began to feel lightheaded; had to remind myself to breathe.

"Who are you?" William demanded.

"He's a friend of mine." Tanisha boldly stepped next to me.

William wouldn't be distracted. "How the hell'd you get in here?"

I couldn't take my eyes off that gun. At any second it

7 **unarmed:** unbewaffnet

might go off. Even if it was an accident it wouldn't matter.

"I let him in," Tanisha said.

"The hell you did," William returned. "You were in the den botherin' me about the weather."

"No, I meant before you came home," Tanisha quickly explained.

William lowered the gun. As the barrel went down my eyes went up, past the string of green and yellow beads around his neck, to his face. He was broad-shouldered and I knew I'd seen him before, but it took a second to remember where. That day behind King Chicken with Lightbulb and Snoop. William was the one who'd hit the old guy in the face with the butt of his gun, and nearly shot Snoop.

I saw a glimmer in William's eye and quickly looked away, but it was too late. "I know you?" he asked.

Staring at the floor, I shook my head.

"Yeah, I do," William said. "I seen you before." He turned to Tanisha. "Where's he from?"

"School," Tanisha answered.

5 **den:** Wohnzimmer 8 **barrel:** Pistolenlauf

"Yeah, but where he *from*?"

We both knew what he meant. I didn't want Tanisha to have to say it, so I did. "Douglass."

William cursed and started to raise the gun again.

"How old are you?"

"Fourteen."

"Know any Disciples?"

I nodded. It would have been stupid to lie. You couldn't live in Douglass and not know someone from the gang. By now the gun was level with my eyes.

"You can't shoot him!" Tanisha cried.

"Not here," her brother answered ominously. Keeping the gun on me, he shifted his eyes toward his sister. "How stupid can you possibly be? What do you think would happen if word got out you was seein' some boy from Douglass?" William swung his head back and forth in disbelief. "Might as well line me up in front of a firin' squad."

"Please let him go," Tanisha begged.

"You ever gonna see him again?" William asked.

I should have seen the question coming, but it caught

12 **ominous:** bedrohlich, unheilvoll 18 **firing squad:** Exekutionskommando

us both by surprise. Tanisha's mouth fell open, but no words came out.

"Well?" William demanded. "Say it before I put a cap in this punk's ass."

A tear spilled out of Tanisha's eye and rolled down her cheek. She hung her head. "I won't."

"Won't what?"

"Won't see him again." Tanisha let out an anguished cry and rushed back into the den.

William kept the gun trained on me. "When you go, keep your head down. Don't let anyone get a good look at you. Go straight back to Douglass. And so help me, I ever see you on this side of town again ... I ever *hear* you come close to my sister again, I will hunt you down and kill you sure as the sun will rise."

4 **cap:** Kugel **punk:** Mistkerl 8 **anguished:** gequält

Twenty-one

Nia banged on the bathroom door. "Open up now, Kalon!"

"Just a second." The lock was broken and I had my foot jammed against the bottom of the door, keeping it closed.

"I'm gonna tell Gramma what you're doing," Nia threatened.

"Go ahead." The truth was, I was shaving my upper lip. I didn't have any hair growing there yet, but I'd heard if you shaved, it made the hair grow in faster.

Nia banged again. "Come on! I gotta go!"

"Another second." I rinsed the razor and put it back in the medicine cabinet, then wiped my face with a towel to get rid of any telltale shaving cream.

19 **to rinse:** abspülen 21 **telltale:** verräterisch

When I opened the door, Nia looked around suspiciously and took a deep sniff.

She grabbed the towel off the rack and buried her face in it. She looked up, puzzled at first, but that quickly changed. "Shaving cream!"

I felt my face turn hot.

A triumphant smile flashed across my sister's lips. "Well, keep your fingers crossed and with luck you'll be shaving by the time you're twenty-one, baby face," she said. "Now get out of here and let me do my business."

I left the bathroom. The door to the bedroom was open. It was one of those rare, quiet moments when both babies were asleep. Denzel was sitting on the corner of the bed with a small paintbrush in his hand. He'd placed half a dozen little jars of paint on the floor and was carefully painting a small action figure holding a sword.

"What is it?" I whispered, not wanting to wake the babies.

"Warhammer," Denzel answered. He pointed at a

4 **puzzled:** verwirrt 8 **to keep one's fingers crossed:** die Daumen drücken

small black plastic case which lay open by his feet. Inside the case, a dozen painted figures of knights with shields, swords and spears were nestled in gray foam.

"You painted all of them?" I asked.

Denzel nodded. "I play over at the hobby center."

"Play?"

"It's a strategy game. We have armies that fight each other. I'll show you sometime."

Fighting armies? We had them all around us. I decided not to reply and headed into the den. Gramma was watching *Judge Brown*. Her gray hair poked out unevenly and she had bags under her eyes. Seemed like lately she was going to work less and spending more time sitting on that old couch. Used to be she'd get dressed up and go out on the weekends more, too. But then, she was 49, and that was real old.

Down in the lobby, Terrell was drinking a bottle of malt liquor and sitting on an old car seat some guys had dragged inside. He offered the bottle to me, and I took a drink.

2 **knight:** Ritter **shield:** Schild 3 **spear:** Speer
3 **to nestle:** eingebettet sein, sich hineinkuscheln **foam:** Schaumstoff 11 **unevenly:** ungleichmäßig

"Gonna go play some C-Low," he said. "Want to come?"

"No money," I said.

"You can watch."

Ever since that day at King Chicken when Marcus had slapped him around, Terrell had been changing. He just forced himself to get tougher, and meaner, and angrier. He always had gambling and drinking money now. Not what guys called "real" money, like enough to buy a car or even a flat-screen TV. But enough to make life a little more interesting than before.

"Who're you shooting with?" I asked.

"Bublz and some friend of his." Terrell gestured towards the door. "Here they come."

Bublz's friend was stocky and ominous-looking. He was wearing a black knit cap.

"This is my second cousin, Jules," said Bublz proudly, like he was glad to be related to someone so tough.

"Where you from?" Terrell asked, not getting up or offering to shake hands.

"Here." He cracked his knuckles. "Just moved in."

1 **C-Low:** Würfelspiel, die Kombination 4-5-6 ist der bestmögliche Wurf 6 **to slap:** schlagen 7 **mean:** gemein, fies
21 **to crack one's knuckles:** die Fingerknöchel zum Knacken bringen

Terrell smirked. "Like it?"

But Jules didn't get it. He made a face. "You serious? It's worse than ghetto." He looked around impatiently as if he wasn't interested in chit chat. "So where you want to play?"

"In the back," said Terrell, slowly hoisting himself to his feet, trying to look as tough as he could. We went down a hall and out a back door. A security light above the door would provide illumination. A couple of kids were spraying tags on the wall, but now that Terrell was a Disciple, all he had to say was "Get lost," and they scattered like roaches.

Terrell, Bublz, and Jules kneeled down and started to roll. Terrell and Jules were quiet and intense, working hard to outpose each other, while Bublz jabbered nervously in that high voice. I stared out into the dark and smoked some bud. The more I smoked, the less sharp and jagged missing Tanisha felt. Every sound around me seemed amplified. The clickity clack rolling of the green and red dice, the hopeful mutterings of the guys, followed by disappointed grunts or triumphant chortles, the

2 **to get it:** (ugs.) verstehen 4 **chit chat:** Smalltalk
6 **to hoist sth.:** etw. hochziehen 9 **illumination:** Beleuchtung
15 **to jabber:** brabbeln 17 **bud:** (ugs.) Hasch
19 **amplified:** verstärkt **clickity clack:** klackernd
21 **chortle:** grunzendes, halb verschlucktes Lachen

traffic, the angry couple yelling from a window somewhere above. It all came together in the chorus of the projects.

I closed my eyes. There'd once been a different music in my ears. Back in the day when Terrell and I had been shorties and we used to play box ball, cops and robbers, tag, and hide and seek. It was a chorus of laughter and shouting. There were gangs and shootings back then, too. But they didn't mean anything to us. They were just short interruptions in the fun.

Crash! The smashing of a bottle snapped me back. Jules had tossed it out into the dark. "I'm sick of playin' for a dollar or two," he grumbled in a voice that sounded syrupy from the drinking and weed. "Who wants to make it five and ten?"

Terrell's eyes were glazed, and his movements were slow, but there was no way he was backing down. "Sure. Five and ten."

Bublz backed away while Jules and Terrell rolled. Soon there must have been close to $80 lying on the ground and Jules was shaking the dice. He had to roll a

6 **box ball:** Schulhofspiel **cops and robbers:** Räuber und Gendarm 7 **tag:** Fangen **hide and seek:** Verstecken
11 **to snap s.o. back:** jmd. aus seinen Träumen reißen
14 **syrupy:** träge

six. He swung his arm down and the dice skipped against the ground and ricocheted off the brick wall. I could have sworn he'd rolled a three, but an instant later his hand swept down, scattering the dice.

"I won," he said, scooping up the bills.

"Bullcrap," Terrell said. "You rolled a three,"

"A six." Jules got to his feet and shoved the money in his pocket. He stumbled backward a step and waved his arms as if having trouble with his balance.

"A three." Terrell rose unsteadily.

They glared at each other. I got up, feeling woozy, but alert to the growing sense of danger. The music of the night drained away.

"Where you goin' anyway?" Terrell asked.

"I gotta fade," Jules said.

"The hell you do," Terrell snarled.

"Hey," Bublz started to say, but Jules cut him off with "Shut up." He glared at Terrell and cracked his knuckles. "You gonna stop me?"

"Give me that money," Terrell said.

Jules was quiet for a moment, as if considering his

2 **to ricochet:** von etw. abprallen 3 **instant:** Augenblick
4 **to scatter:** verstreuen 6 **bullcrap:** völlige Scheiße
7 **to shove:** stopfen 11 **woozy:** duselig im Kopf
15 **I gotta fade:** Ich muss los

options. Then he turned to Bublz. "You tell him. It was a six, right?"

Bublz's eyes darted frantically between his cousin and his friend. He lowered his gaze. "I didn't see."

"Did you see?" Terrell asked me.

I nodded. "Looked like a three."

"Well, you're wrong. It was a six." Jules puffed out his chest.

"You ain't goin' nowhere," Terrell threatened. I'd never seen him this angry. Suddenly he started to wheeze and reached into his starter jacket to get the inhaler.

Jules grinned. "Some tough guy."

Terrell slid his hand inside the starter jacket again. But this time it didn't come out. "Give back the money, or else."

I felt a chill. Jules stared at the spot where Terrell's hand disappeared into his jacket. His lips parted into a grin. "Or what? You gonna shoot me with your inhaler?"

Terrell took a small, black pistol out of his pocket. It was a .22.

3 **frantically:** hektisch, verzweifelt 7 **to puff out:** rausstrecken, aufblasen 11 **starter jacket:** Sportjacke mit dem Logo eines Vereins

"Oh, no," Bublz whimpered and backed away. Jules didn't move. He stared at the gun. "You ain't got the guts."

"Give the money back,"

"Give it back, Jules." Bublz's voice was trembling. "He's a Disciple,"

"I don't care if he's the NBA, FBI and NFL," Jules spit.

"You will when you sober up."

Jules ignored his cousin. "He don't have the guts. Probably don't even know how to use that thing. I bet it ain't even loaded."

"This is the last time I'm gonna say it." Terrell warned. "Give me that money."

Jules cursed him.

Bang!

Bublz and I jumped. Jules went down with a thud. "My foot!" he cried. "You shot my foot!"

"You're lucky I didn't shoot your face," Terrell said.

Jules lay on his side on the ground, clutching his foot. Tears squeezed out of the corners of his eyes. Terrell bent

3 **guts:** Mut 7 **NBA:** (kurz für "National Basketball Association") landesweite Basketball-Liga **FBI:** (kurz für "Federal Bureau of Investigation") amerikanische Bundespolizei **NFL:** (kurz für "National Football League") Profiliga des American Football
9 **to sober up:** ausnüchtern 20 **to clutch:** umklammern

over Jules and started to go through his pockets, searching for the money.

Wham! Jules swung his arm out hard, catching Terrell square in the face. My friend fell back and the pistol clattered to the ground about five feet from where Jules lay. Jules rose to his hands and knees. He looked at the gun, then he looked at me.

And just like that, I knew what he was thinking.

He lunged for the gun. For a kid who'd just been shot in the foot, he moved pretty fast.

But I was faster, scooping up the gun and aiming it down at him. Still on his hands and knees, Jules looked up at the gun I was pointing into his face. This was the first time I'd ever held a real gun, and even though it was small, it weighed more than I'd expected. My heart was hammering and my hand trembled, but I willed it to stop.

Then, out of nowhere, a different sensation took hold. With that gun in my hand I began to feel powerful in a way I'd never felt before. Like I was a real badass and could make anyone fear me.

4 **square in the face:** mitten im Gesicht 5 **to clatter:** klappern (hier: scheppernd fallen) 9 **to lunge for sth.:** sich auf etw. stürzen 20 **badass:** Fiesling

Terrell rose unsteady to his feet and staggered toward me with his hand out. "Gimme."

"No," I said.

"I said, gimme!" Terrell demanded.

Keeping Jules in the corner of my eye, I swung my arm around and aimed the gun at Terrell.

"What?" Terrell's mouth fell open. Then his face scrunched up like he didn't understand. "You …" He squinted his eyes. "Whose side you on?"

"Yours, stupid."

I aimed the gun at Jules. "Keep your hands where I can see them. Bublz, take forty dollars out of his pocket and give it to Terrell."

Since Terrell and Jules had been playing head on, half the $80 belonged to each of them. Now they were even.

Terrell counted the money and shoved it into his pocket. Then he turned to Jules. "I ever see you around here again, I'll kill you soon as look at you." He disappeared into the building.

Jules sat up, holding his foot and moaning. His sneaker and hands were all red. Bublz squatted next to him.

8 **to scrunch up:** zusammenziehen, sich in Falten legen
9 **to squint:** Augen zusammenkneifen

"Take him to the emergency room," I said. "Tell them you and him were playing around with a gun and it went off accidentally."

I bent down in front of Jules. "Know what happens to snitches?"

He didn't respond.

Slap! I smacked him half-hard in the face. "Answer me."

Jules jerked up his head, gritting his teeth venomously. "I know."

Straightening up, I said to Bublz, "They're gonna try to get you to change your story, but no matter what they say, you stick to it. You tell anyone what really happened and …"

"Don't have to tell me." Bublz helped his cousin up. Jules grimaced and draped his arm over Bublz's shoulder for support. But he narrowed his eyes and gave me a look to let me know that if I wasn't holding that gun, he'd kill me with his bare hands.

I waited until they left, then went out to the street and threw the gun down a storm drain.

5 **snitch:** Petze, Verräter 9 **venomously:** giftig
16 **to drape:** hängen 21 **storm drain:** Gully

The next day I didn't bother to go to school. I was lazing around and watching TV when Denzel came out of the bedroom buckling his belt. "Get dressed," he said.

I didn't have to ask why. A little while later I was on the fifteenth floor for the first time since the day two years before when Marcus gave me his bail money. In the middle of a filthy room, Jules was kneeling with his hands bound behind him and his eyes blindfolded. His lower lip was swollen and split, and his nose was caked with blood. His left foot was wrapped in a bandage so I knew he'd made it to the emergency room the night before.

Marcus and Terrell were there, along with Tyrone.

"Where's the gun?" Marcus asked me.

"Threw it down a storm drain," I said.

"What!?" Terrell sputtered.

Marcus gave him a silencing look, then turned to me. "Smart. Cops can't prove nothing without a weapon." He gestured at Jules. "He cheat?"

I glanced at the blindfolded, cowering figure. "He's new around here and made a mistake. We were all pretty wasted."

3 **to buckle:** zuschnallen 8 **blindfolded:** verbunden
9 **split:** aufgeplatzt 18 **to cheat:** schummeln, betrügen
21 **wasted:** hinüber (besoffen, bekifft)

"So you don't think we should kill him?" Marcus asked with a wink.

Jules shuddered.

"Hell, no," I said. "In fact, I think he'd make a pretty good Disciple."

"Over my dead body," Terrell snorted.

"Don't ever say that," Tyrone muttered. "Unless you want it to come true."

2 **wink:** Zwinkern

FIFTEEN YEARS OLD

Many inner-city children grow up without parental guidance. It is not uncommon to find 12-year-olds who cannot read. In some gang areas in California only five out of one hundred students reach the required standard in mathematics or English.

Twenty-two

"Kalon, wake up." Someone was shaking my shoulder. I opened my eyes. In the dim light Denzel crouched over me. On the couch Gramma made a snorting noise and rolled over without opening her eyes.

"S'up?" I yawned, rising to my elbows from my small mattress on the floor.

"Something's going on."

I pushed off my blanket and got up. Denzel pulled back the heavy green curtains and we looked out. It was March and heavy gray clouds were leaving a fine mist in the air. Parked along Abernathy Ave were shiny new cars and white vans with News 8 and Eyewitness News written on their sides. Down in the yard camera crews and reporters were interviewing people.

10 **snorting:** grunzend, schnarchend 17 **mist:** Nebel

"What is it?" I asked, pulling on some clothes.

"Don't know but it must be big," said Denzel.

Nia came out of the bedroom with one baby on each hip, both of them sucking their thumbs. "You goin' out?" she asked Denzel. Lately, she almost always sounded annoyed when she spoke to him.

"Maybe."

"Then maybe you won't forget the Pampers this time."

Denzel rolled his eyes. The more Nia nagged, the quieter he grew. Nia's eyebrows slanted down and she looked mad. She was always complaining that Denzel didn't help enough and that she never had time to do anything for herself or see her friends.

"You better not come back without those Pampers," she warned him.

But Denzel didn't care to answer and left.

I followed him down to the lobby, were Terrell, Jamar, and Marcus were talking in a corner by the broken elevator. Marcus waved Denzel over while I continued outside. Despite a cold, wet mist that left a silvery sheen

10 **to nag:** nörgeln, meckern

on everyone's clothes and hair, there were a lot of people out in the yard, mostly circling the television cameras with their bright lights and well-dressed reporters.

I ran into Precious, who was shivering and held her jacket closed over her big belly with both hands.

"What's going on?" I asked.

"Two shorties from number three shot a pregnant lady in the belly."

"How old?"

"Nine, ten. They took her to the hospital. People say she'll probably live, but the baby's dead for sure."

So that explained the news crews. They were asking people if they knew the shorties or the lady who got shot. Most of the people who said they did probably didn't. They just wanted to be on TV. Terrell and Denzel came through the crowd.

"Gotta bounce," Denzel said. He reached into his pocket and pulled out some bills. "Do me a favor, okay?" I could have guessed that I would end up buying the Pampers myself.

He'd been promoted to runner. It was his job to de-

17 **gotta bounce:** ich muss weg 21 **runner:** Kurier

liver the money and pick up the drugs souljas like Terrell sold on the street. In some ways it was the most dangerous gang job because so much of the time he was carrying either a lot of money or a lot of drugs.

He took off, leaving Terrell, Precious, and me. Precious gave Terrell a yearning glance. Now that she was pregnant, she wasn't so haughty anymore. Other guys weren't interested in pregnant girls.

"Want to do something?" she asked Terrell.

Terrell gave her a cold look. "No."

Precious pursed her lips, but then she set her jaw hard and left.

"Sure it ain't your kid?" I asked.

"No, but I ain't sure it is, either," Terrell replied.

"Why would she say it was yours if it wasn't?"

"'cause maybe that skank don't know," Terrell said. "Maybe she just thinks I'm the best choice."

"Girls usually know."

"Oh, yeah? Who made you the expert?"

"What if it really is yours?" I asked.

Terrell gave me a disdainful look. "She can't prove

7 **haughty:** hochnäsig 16 **skank:** (ugs.) Schlampe
21 **disdainful:** verächtlich

nothing, okay? And I ain't with her no more. Anyway, I like Imani better."

Imani was a short, slight girl with long, wavy brown hair. She was soft-spoken and shy, almost the opposite of Precious.

"Since when?" I asked.

"Since always." Terrell smiled sheepishly. "And maybe if I'm any baby's daddy, it's hers."

Twenty-three

That night the shooting was the first story on all the news shows. They said doctors had operated to remove the dead baby, and the mother was expected to recover. They didn't show photographs of the shorties who'd shot her, but they did show an old photo of the victim and we all agreed that we'd seen her around. The part Gramma and Nia liked the best was when they interviewed our neighbors about what had happened. They'd interview one person, but crowds of others would be around them, all trying to get their faces on TV.

It was like that on every channel. If people we knew weren't the ones being interviewed, then we could pick them out of the crowd. It was strangely exciting to see everyday people like us on the same screen that showed the most famous stars and rappers and athletes on earth.

But the fun didn't last. Next the mayor came on and spoke about the shooting as a tragedy, and how not one, but three lives had been wasted – the woman's unborn child, and the two boys as well. He asked what kind of world it was where children shot mothers-to-be.

The camera moved to an important-looking police commander standing next to the mayor. He said they were investigating rumors that the boys were part of the Douglass Disciples.

"That's a damn lie," Denzel spat. "I never saw those shorties before."

The camera went back to the mayor, who promised there'd be more police enforcement around Frederick Douglass. Then some commercials came on.

"Good," said Gramma. "Now let's watch something nice."

"No," I said, getting up.

Everyone looked surprised. Usually I was the last person to make a fuss about what was on the TV. I turned

21 **to make a fuss:** einen Aufstand machen

to a show where three women in dresses and two men in suits were sitting around a table discussing the shooting.

One of the women and one of the men was dark-skinned. The black man wore a red bow tie.

“That looks stupid,” said Nia uncomfortably, as if she sensed that, other than the color of his skin, he had nothing in common with us.

One of the white men asked the black man with the bow tie how he thought something like the shooting could happen.

“Hear that?” Nia said. “He’s makin’ it sound like he thinks something like this could never happen in his white world.”

“The projects are a lost, hidden and forgotten world that most people don’t even know exists,” the black man said.

“Or don’t want to know exists,” added the black woman. “It’s a hopeless cycle of broken families, illegitimate children, failed education, poverty, and lawlessness.”

The twins sat on the floor sucking their thumbs, staring at the images on the TV. They couldn't have understood, but the rest of us in that cramped, hot little room did. This was our world they were talking about. We were that broken family living on welfare and food stamps, with illegitimate children and school drop outs and gang members.

"They may look black, but they talk white," Gramma said, as if that would somehow negate what was being said.

"Not one of them ever set foot in the projects, that's for sure," muttered Nia.

"Let's face it," said one of the white women on the TV. "It's survival of the fittest. Those who survive do so by their wits and pure animal instincts. It's the rule of the jungle. The asphalt jungle. The projects are a dumping ground for society's rejects. They're the last stop on the backward slide into barbarianism."

"I've had enough. Dumbheads, all of them," Nia said.

Denzel got up and turned the TV off. The room went

9 **negate:** nichtig machen 15 **wits:** Köpfchen, Cleverness
16 **dumping ground:** Müllhalde 17 **reject:** zu nichts zu gebrauchender Rest

quiet. From outside came the distant sounds of traffic, rap music, and the screech of train wheels in the rail yard.

Asphalt jungle ...

A dumping ground ...

Rejects ...

"Give it here." Gramma gestured for the clicker. She turned the TV back to some comedy. The laugh track filled the room.

But none of us laughed.

Twenty-four

By day politicians and other important people came to make speeches in front of television cameras about how they were going to rehabilitate the Frederick Douglass Projects. But as soon as the sun went down and the reporters went home for dinner, it was the old thing. Gunfire, fear, isolation.

"You believe that crap?" Terrell said on yet another night while we watched some white windbag talk about what he was gonna do for us underprivileged, uneducated, uncivilized folks. "They ain't gonna do nothing."

"Maybe they will," I said.

"Then why ain't there politicians over at Gentry talking about what they're gonna do there?" Terrell asked. "Or at Pierpont Plaza or Freemont-McClaren?"

10 **rehabilitate:** wieder in die Gesellschaft eingliedern
14 **crap:** Scheiße 15 **windbag:** (ugs.) Schwätzer

"'cause they ain't got no nine-year-old killers over there," said Gramma, bouncing Jayda on her knee.

"Damn right," Terrell said as if this proved his point. "If they was gonna do something about the projects, they'd be talkin' 'bout *all* the projects. Not just Douglass. They're just using those kids as an excuse to get on TV and mouth off."

Nia came into the room with Xavier on her hip, her cell phone against her ear, and a frown on her face. "Any idea where Denzel is? He always answers when I call. Always."

Terrell shrugged his shoulders. "I could check a few spots."

"Why don't you do that," Nia said. "And if you find him, tell him to call home right away, hear?"

When Terrell and I got out into the hall, he said we had to go upstairs first. There must have been half a dozen Disciples milling around on the fifteenth floor, including Bublz, Jules and Darius who'd become a Disciple a few weeks before. The chin of the latter was propped in his hand and he was writing in a battered spiral notebook.

7 **to mouth off:** die Klappe aufreißen 18 **to mill around:** herumlaufen 21 **battered:** zerknautscht, abgegriffen

That at least reminded me of the Darius I knew before, who was either mimicking *50 Cent* while listening to some scratchy hip hop on his boombox, or you would find him writing some angry verse about "fucking ghetto life." Maybe he thought that being a Disciple would help him on his way up and out of here. Or at least provide him with the necessary money or bling.

Tension was thick in the air and gang members were speaking in hushed, hurried voices.

We went into Marcus's apartment. Marcus, Jamar and Tyrone were standing around the kitchen table, which was covered with guns and boxes of ammunition.

"When'd you last see Denzel?" Marcus asked me.

"This morning," I said.

"Was he strapped?"

I shrugged. "Didn't notice. He usually is."

"We gotta squad up and spill some blood," Jamar said. "They want a war, they'll get a war."

Marcus shared a look with Tyrone and Jamar.

"We need to know for certain first," Marcus replied grimly. "He ain't even late yet."

9 **hushed:** leise, gedämpft 15 **strapped:** (ugs.) bewaffnet
17 **to squad up:** sich zusammenrotten

"Come on, man, that's bull and you know it," Jamar said. "Denzel ain't here. He ain't answerin' his phone. Where do you think he's at?"

"Someplace else," Marcus barked. "Maybe he stopped to see a girlfriend. Maybe he got pinched. Maybe he got ambushed by a crew that ain't Gentry. You want to start a war with the wrong enemy?"

"Gentry's the enemy no matter what," Jamar said.

Marcus frowned, then opened a flip phone and dialed it. The room grew quiet. Marcus let the phone ring five times then snapped it shut.

"You each take a man and go look for him," he told Jamar and Tyrone. "Soon as you know anything, you call me."

"You want me to look, too?" Terrell asked eagerly.

"I want you to sit on that bench and do what you're supposed to do," Marcus said, clearly annoyed.

"But ..."

Marcus glared at him sharply and Terrell didn't finish the sentence. When we passed the third floor on our way downstairs, I turned toward Gramma's, but Terrell

4 **to bark:** bellen, brüllen 5 **pinched:** (ugs.) verhaftet
9 **flip phone:** Klapphandy

grabbed my arm. “Come on, Kalon. We’re gonna find Denzel.”

“But Marcus said …”

“Marcus wants me to grow old and die on that bench,” Terrell hissed. “I’m gonna show him I’m better than that. Maybe the Gangstas ain’t got Denzel. Maybe he knows they’re lookin’ for him and he’s hiding. Maybe we can find him before they do. Your sister Nia asked me to find him, right?”

I nodded.

Terrell patted me on the shoulder. “Then that’s what we’re gonna do. We got each other’s backs, Kalon. Long as we stick together we’ll be okay.”

Outside the night air was chilly. Winter wasn’t quite ready to give up and let spring in. Terrell started walking west, toward the Flats.

“Why this way?” I asked.

“The hobby center,” Terrell said. “You know, he plays this Warhammer game and don’t want anyone to know, so he turns off his phone.”

12 **We got each other’s backs:** Wir halten uns gegenseitig den Rücken frei

Suddenly I remembered that when Denzel had left the apartment that morning, he'd had that black plastic case with him. Relief filtered through me.

I'd been scared that my sister was gonna lose her man, and, like so many of us, those babies would never know their father.

Terrel entered the hobby center as if he owned the place. Everything stopped.

They recognized his colors.

"Anyone seen a guy named Denzel?" Terrell asked.

"Who?" someone asked back.

"Medium size, long braids, diamond stud in his right ear," I explained.

"He was here," a guy said. "Probably left ten minutes ago."

Terrell and I shared a puzzled look. If Denzel left, why hadn't we run into him on the way over?

"Was he with anyone?" I asked.

The guys exchanged glances and head shakes. Terrell jerked his head and we left the store.

13 **stud:** Ohrstecker

At the sound of the gunshot, we both ducked. Car doors slammed and a low gray car shot out of an alley next to the hobby shop and sped away. We ran into the alley. In the shadows a body lay on the ground. My heart started to race and I slowed down as if part of me didn't want to know. But I knew. Denzel's hands were tied behind him and he lay curled up as if he'd been kneeling when they shot him. A single bullet through the back of his head. I felt something under my foot. Black and white beads were scattered on the ground. It was the Gangsta's way of letting us know who pulled the trigger.

Terrell cursed, and I heard beeps as he dialed a number. Part of Denzel's forehead was gone. Even in death his eyes were squeezed shut. My head started to throb.

"He knew what was coming," I muttered.

"Huh?" Terrell didn't understand.

"Look at his eyes. He knew they were gonna kill him. They made him kneel."

In the dim light, something glistened on Denzel's cheek. I reached down and touched the moisture. It wasn't blood. It was tears. He'd been crying when they

2 **alley:** Gasse 11 **trigger:** Abzug

shot him. The throbbing in my head grew into pounding. I saw Xavier's and Jayda's small faces. Nia's expectant eyes.

A car pulled into the alley. "Crap!" Thinking it might be Gentry, Terrell pulled his gun and shielded his eyes. Car doors opened.

I heard the footsteps, but didn't look up. Terrell backed away and I felt a shadow as Marcus stood over me silently. The pain made my head throb like it was going to explode. I felt my hands clench. "You killed him!" I launched myself at Marcus.

The scuffle was short. In no time Marcus had me tied up with his strong arms and hands. But I was still fighting, squirming and cursing. "It's your fault! You made him a runner! You got him killed!"

"Chill. Calm down." Marcus held me tightly.

"Go to hell!"

Marcus increased his grip, pinning my arms to my sides. I heard him say, "Put those guns away."

I opened my eyes. Jules and two other gangbangers had their guns out, ready to kill me if I did anything to

1 **pounding:** dumpfes Hämmern 12 **scuffle:** Handgemenge

Marcus. They hesitated, then put the guns away. I tried to twist out of Marcus's grip, but his hands were like steel clamps cutting off the circulation to my arms.

"What do you want us to do?" Jules asked.

Marcus nodded at Denzel's body. "Go, search his pockets."

"Don't touch him!" I started to fight anew. "Leave him alone!"

Marcus clamped a hand over my mouth. I twisted and tried to get free, but he put an arm around my chest and squeezed until it was hard to breathe. Jules went through Denzel's pockets and came up with a couple of crumpled dollar bills and a cell phone.

"Give it here." Still holding me with one hand, Marcus took the phone. For a split second his gaze settled on Terrell, and a frown formed on his face. "All of you, get out of here."

Jules nodded at me. "What about him?"

"He's going with me," Marcus said.

"The hell I am!" Once again I tried to fight, but Marcus pushed me face first down on the cold wet pavement

3 **clamp:** Klemme **circulation:** Blutfluss

and twisted my arm behind my back. "That's enough," he grunted and held me down until the others had gone. I felt his breath close to my ear. "I'm gonna let you go and you ain't gonna do nothing stupid, you understand?"

When I didn't answer he twisted my arm harder and I felt the pain shoot up through my shoulder like it was going to pop out of the joint. "Understand?" he growled again.

Trembling and seized with pain from my shoulder, I nodded. "I understand."

Marcus let go. "Get in the car," he ordered.

I pushed myself up from the ground and looked at Denzel's body. "You're just gonna leave him like that?"

"I said, get in the car."

I did as I was told. Marcus looked over the backseat as he backed the Mercedes out of the alley. He drove about half a block and pulled over. I watched silently while he dialed 911 on Denzel's phone.

"There's a body in the alley on the nine hundred block of Whitmore," he told the operator. "The deceased's

8 **joint:** Gelenk 10 **seized:** gelähmt 20 **body:** Leiche
21 **deceased:** Toter

name is Denzel Young. His address is Number One, Frederick Douglass, apartment three F," he hung up, got out of the car, and dropped Denzel's phone to the ground. He crushed it with his foot and kicked the pieces into a storm drain.

Getting into the car again, he turned to me and said, "Get this straight. Denzel was a runner because he wanted to be a runner. There's only three ways up – treasurer, enforcer, or runner. We're okay in the treasurer department and Denzel didn't want to be no enforcer, and that's that."

I sat in the front seat, silent, arms crossed. People in this country were supposed to have choices. That's what teachers in school said. And the politicians on TV. But this world here was different. Here there were no choices. No good ones, at least.

I thought Marcus would start the car, but he didn't. "You think Denzel liked livin' in that apartment with you and your gramma? A man wants a crib of his own. He wants a ride and enough bank to keep his babies in Pampers and go out at night if he chooses."

7 **get this straight:** pass auf; damit eins klar ist.
8 **treasurer:** Schatzmeister

"What happens to my sister and her babies now?" I asked.

Marcus drummed his fingers against the steering wheel, then reached into his pocket and pulled out a wad of cash. He thumbed off a bunch of bills and handed them to me. "Give this to your sister."

The distant wail of a siren broke the silence. Marcus looked into the rearview mirror. A cop car with flashing lights came up the block and turned down the alley. Marcus started the car and we drove away.

"How come you waited?" I asked.

"Wanted to make sure the right people found the body."

Twenty-five

No stories about the execution-style murder of a 17-year-old gangbanger appeared on TV or in the newspapers. No politicians made speeches. But two weeks later, when a blond 18-year-old college freshman disappeared in Mexico while on spring break with friends, it was all over the TV for days until she was found dazed and dirty, but otherwise okay, on a Cancun street corner.

Gramma's funeral insurance paid for the funeral. She didn't have life or health or any other kind of insurance, but every month she paid $48 to cover the cost of a funeral in case anyone in the family died. When Nia became pregnant, she'd added Denzel to the policy. In her mind the worst and most undignified thing that could happen was to be buried in Potter's Field, the place

11 **college freshman:** Student(in) im ersten Studienjahr
13 **dazed:** benommen 15 **insurance:** Versicherung

where the city put the lost souls who had no families or money for "a proper" burial.

Nia was all broken up over Denzel. She stayed in bed and cried for days while Gramma and I took care of the twins. After a week she went down to social services and applied for support, but they said it would be months before the paperwork came through. So each day she left the babies with Gramma and went upstairs where Marcus gave her a job processing drugs.

Then Gramma came down with shingles. We had to prop her up on the couch with pillows. The disease gave her blisters on her face and arms, but the worst part was the pain. She'd wince and moan, "Oh, Lord, oh, Lord," over and over. We knew it was bad because usually she never complained about anything. It was so bad that she didn't even care about watching *Judge Brown*.

After three days I went down to get some medicine that would help. I strolled down Abernathy Avenue, taking my time, breathing in the first signs of springtime. The sun was out and the air felt warm and moist. There

10 **to come down with sth.:** eine Krankheit bekommen
shingles: Gürtelrose 12 **blister:** Blase 21 **moist:** feucht

were even some robins hopping around the yard, trying to pull worms out of the dirt. I had almost reached the clinic when Lightbulb came in the other direction with his head bowed and a sad look in his eyes.

"What's wrong?" I asked.

He looked up, surprised, then hung his head. "Snoop's gone."

I'd never seen Lightbulb this down.

"I'm on my way to the clinic," I told him. "Want to come?"

Lightbulb shook his head. "I'm gonna keep looking."

"Okay. Hope you find him."

I picked up Gramma's medicine. On the way out of the clinic I noticed a beat-up old white Cadillac Seville across the street. A skinny hype girl got out. It was morning and she was wearing a short skirt and red high heels and lots of make-up so you knew what she did to support her habit. I started to look away and then did a double take. It was Laqueta.

She crossed the street, her ankles all wobbly and un-

1 **robin:** Rotkehlchen 19 **to support a habit:** Drogensucht finanzieren 20 **to do a double take:** zweimal hinsehen

steady in those red high heels, and went through the special clinic door where junkies got their methadone. Meanwhile, the Seville stayed parked with its motor running. It was one sorry-looking vehicle. The red fabric on the roof was torn back, one fender crushed in and missing a headlight, an old sun-bleached For Sale sign in the rear window.

Laqueta came out of the clinic and crossed the street. Only she didn't get back into the car. She leaned in the window and handed the driver a small bottle of red liquid. In return he slid her some dead presidents.

The car pulled away. Laqueta looked across the street and our eyes met. Her eyebrows dropped as she recognized me and probably realized I'd seen what she'd just done. She raised one eyebrow and licked her red lips. I turned away and headed home.

Back at the apartment I gave Gramma her medicine and then went out to the yard. I needed to talk to Terrell. He was in his usual spot on the bench.

"S'up?" he said.

"Just saw Laqueta down at the clinic."

4 **sorry-looking:** übel aussehend, völlig fertig **fabric:** Stoff
5 **fender:** Kotflügel 6 **headlight:** Scheinwerfer
sun-bleached: ausgeblichen 10 **liquid:** Flüssigkeit
11 **dead presidents:** Geldscheine

"Oh, yeah?" Terrell sounded less than interested.

"Sellin' her methadone."

Terrell gave me a wary look, but said nothing.

"She's a hype now?" I asked.

Terrell bristled. "She's had a very hard time, okay? Her little boy fell out that window and Jamar dumped her."

"So that makes it okay?"

"No, it don't make it okay," said Terrell. "I'm just sayin', that's all."

"Know what else she's doing?"

Terrell narrowed his eyes. "What is this?"

"I'm just asking if you know what your cousin's doing for drug money," I said.

Terrell's jaw hardened. "Yeah. What's your point?"

I stared at him. "Don't you get it? What're you doing on this bench?"

"You know what I'm doing."

"You think Laqueta'd be a junky hooker right now if it wasn't for gangbangers like you out here sellin' dope?"

5 **to bristle:** ärgerlich werden 19 **hooker:** Nutte

"What she does is her business," Terrell muttered with a shrug.

But I was still in his face. "No, man, it's *your* business. You're the one making money while she's out selling herself. And for what? So you can get a little bling? Go to a club on Saturday night and find some new skank to get pregnant?"

Terrell cursed me and we glared at each other. We were lifelong friends. The only real friend each other had. But lately I'd begun to wonder. "This is cold-blooded, Terrell. You're makin' money off your own people. Off your own family, for God's sake."

"Maybe I ain't as high and mighty as you, okay?" Terrell shot back. "Laqueta's grown up enough to make her own decisions. Meanwhile I'm tryin' to work my way up. Because it's either this or workin' at King Chicken with my peeps comin' in and laughin' at me. And I don't know what you think you're doin' that's any better."

"What I'm *not* doin' is sellin' the same drugs my cousin's addicted to," I said.

13 **to be high and mighty:** abgehoben sein

"And what *are* you doin' instead, school boy?" Terrell sneered. "Gonna stay in Munson until you graduate? And then what? Get yourself a job workin' in some factory? Or drivin' a dirty truck? With guys like Marcus makin' more in a day than you make in a month? Wait a minute, school boy. How come you ain't in school today?"

"I had to go to the clinic and get my gramma some medicine."

"So? The day ain't over. You can still go."

He was right. And the truth was, I wasn't at school because I didn't feel like going. Besides, school wasn't leading anywhere. Most of the time I only went there to see Tanisha. More and more I couldn't connect what the things they were teaching us had to do with life. What difference did it make that the Earth was on tectonic plates that sometimes moved and caused earthquakes and tsunamis? There were no earthquakes around here. Who cared what dead guys like Mark Twain and Shakespeare wrote?

Terrell raised his hand in an offer of truce. Maybe he

21 **truce:** Waffenstillstand

was right. All of us were stuck here, just trying to get by. He took out a pinner, lit it and offered me some. I took a hit. Sometimes it was the only way to cope.

"Face it, Kalon," Terrell wheezed as he exhaled sweet smoke. "This is all there is."

2 **pinner:** Minijoint

Twenty-six

"Been a long time since we went out somewhere," Tanisha whispered in my ear. We were lying on a mattress on the floor of an abandoned building near Munson High. Kids used the place all the time to skip school, get high, and hook up. The mattress was filthy and stank, but Tanisha kept clean sheets hidden in a garbage bag in a hole in the wall.

"We go out and get seen, I get killed," I whispered back, stroking her cheek.

"Only around here," she said. "We could meet downtown. Or on the South Side where nobody knows us."

For months the only places she and I had been together were school and this drafty old building with boarded up windows, and broken glass and garbage all

12 **to hook up:** (ugs.) Sex haben

over the floors. But being seen wasn't the only problem with going out.

"Gramma's sick and Nia's welfare checks ain't started yet," I said. "We're already behind on the rent and cable."

"I've got money," Tanisha said. "All those nights I can't see you, I babysit."

I felt my heart twist. Most girls wouldn't put up with a guy without money. Tanisha was different and what we shared was special. Special enough for me to risk my life to see her.

"What's for dinner?" Gramma asked from the couch. Even with the medicine she could hardly move without pain, so it was up to Nia and me to cook.

"Let me check," I said, even though I knew there was hardly anything. The money Marcus had given us was gone. The night before we'd had rice and catsup for dinner, and at least once a day Nia gave the twins sugar water instead of formula.

I went into the kitchen. Nia was standing beside the

5 **cable:** Kabel(fernsehgebühren) 18 **catsup:** (ugs.) Ketchup

counter, her head titled back and eyes closed, gulping something from a can in her hand. She finished with a sigh of satisfaction, then opened her eyes, saw me, and quickly hid the can behind her back.

Her face flushed. What could she be hiding? Had she become a wino without me noticing? Knowing there was no sense in pretending, she brought her hand out from behind her back and placed the can on the counter. It was baby formula.

"Don't tell Gramma," she whispered, her eyes brimming with tears of shame. "I was so hungry."

I saw what I'd missed before. My sister was skinnier than before she'd become pregnant. Her cheeks were hollow and her hands and wrists were bony. I felt an anger rising up from deep inside and turned to leave.

As I went through the living room, Gramma said, "Where're you going?"

"To get some food."

Nia followed me through the front door and out into the hall. "You got money?"

"No," I said. There was the money in the envelope

6 **wino:** Alkoholiker 10 **brimming:** randvoll
14 **wrist:** Handgelenk

Marcus had entrusted to me, but I'd given him my word. Given the choice, I'd rather break the law.

"Then how?"

I turned away and headed downstairs, footsteps slapping, seething with anger, feeling like I wanted to hit someone or something as hard as I could. And that's what I figured I'd have to do, with a rock or a brick. Go down Abernathy a few blocks and wait by the intersection for the right car – one driven by some older white woman with a pocketbook on the seat beside her. Pretend I was crossing with the light and strike fast. Smash the window, grab the bag, and run. Thinking about it made my heart thump hard and my head feel hot. It was a step down to a place I'd tried all my life not to go. But Gramma was sick, and the babies needed food, and we were all very hungry.

Was it fate that I ran into Terrell coming up the stairs? He was wearing a light blue and white University of North Carolina cap backwards with a do-rag under it, a matching over-sized blue and white UNC jersey and basketball shoes, and long denim shorts. He was listen-

5 **to seethe:** kochen 19 **do-rag:** eng anliegende Mütze aus feinstrumpfartigem Material

ing to an iPod, and on his wrist was a gold-plated watch with a thick gold band. Plus he was carrying a shopping bag.

"What'd you get?" I asked.

Terrell took a Nike box out of the bag and opened it. Inside were bright white new basketball shoes. "Nice, huh?"

The blue and white basketball shoes on his feet were hardly scuffed. Meanwhile, I had one pair of sneakers, and I had to keep them fresh with white shoe polish.

"Sup?" he asked.

"Got twenty I can borrow?"

Terrell sneered at me. "End of the month?"

The anger, which had momentarily vanished, came back fast and hard. I felt the urge to say something ugly, but caught myself. "Forget it." I started down the stairs again.

"Whoa," Terrell called behind me. "How about King Chicken? My treat."

I looked back up at him in his new clothes. "Thanks, but I got Nia and Gramma, too."

15 **urge:** dringendes Verlangen 19 **my treat:** Das geht auf meine Rechnung

"Got it covered," Terrell said. "Come on up so I can drop this off."

I didn't move. I didn't want his charity.

"Come on, Kalon. How many times have you saved my sorry butt?"

Next thing I knew, I was climbing the stairs with him.

"Marcus is thinkin' about making me the new runner," he said.

"After what happened to Denzel? You whack?"

"It's good money," Terrell said. "Big step up."

"You'll get yourself killed."

Terrell smirked. "That's the chance you take."

We got up to his apartment. Mrs. Blake wasn't there, but Laqueta and two guys were. The TV was on and the table and floor were covered with bottles and ash trays full of cigarette butts. Laqueta and her friends wore stained, ragged clothes and looked glassy-eyed.

"Gimme some money," Laqueta said languidly, as if she knew he wouldn't.

5 **butt:** Hintern 18 **butt:** Kippe 20 **languidly:** matt, lustlos

Terrell ignored her and went down the hall. His room had a new metal door secured with two padlocks. It was already dented and scratched as if someone had tried to break through. I didn't have to ask who.

Terrell undid the locks. Inside was a flat-screen TV and a new sound system. New clothes with tags still on them were scattered around.

"I thought sitting on the bench didn't pay," I said in a low voice.

"Not till I figured out the system," Terrell answered slyly. "I skim a little off every bag of weed and every vial of rock. Five bags becomes six. Same with the vials. End of the day, the money from the extras is all mine."

"Marcus know?" I asked.

"Probably. Only no one talks about it."

An open bag of peanuts lay on the desk. Terrell saw me eyeing it. "Take as much as you want. My cousins from Georgia send us a new bag practically every month. They must live on the stuff down there."

I took a handful and we left the apartment and walked to King Chicken. It was dinner time and the place was

2 **padlock:** Vorhängeschloss 11 **sly:** schlau, gerissen, hintertrieben **to skim off:** abschöpfen, abzweigen

busy. We got in line and the scent of fried chicken made my stomach grumble.

I was studying the menu overhead when a commotion started in a booth where a heavy lady sat with three shorties. One of the shorties had tipped over a super-sized soda, spilling it all over the table and floor.

"Raydale!" the white-shirted manager yelled back into the kitchen. "Get the mop!"

When Lightbulb came out of the back wearing black pants and a stained white shirt with the tails hanging out, Terrell and I were taken by surprise. He pushed a yellow bucket with a wooden broom handle sticking out of it.

"How long you been working here?" Terrell asked.

"'bout a month," Lightbulb said.

"What about school?" I asked.

Before Lightbulb could answer, the manager yelled again. "Raydale! You gonna talk to your friends?"

Lightbulb hurried toward the booth and started mopping.

"And that?" the woman pointed at the plates, cups and buckets sitting in a sea of soda on the table.

3 **commotion:** Unruhe, Spektakel 10 **tails:** Hemdzipfel

Lightbulb started to wipe the soda off the table, but as he did, it began to spill onto the floor and seats again.

"Watch what you doing!" the woman yelled.

Her yelling flustered Lightbulb, who hated loud noises and anger. In a panic, Lightbulb swiped the towel across the table, splashing some of the soda on the woman's son's pants and shoes.

"Now look what you done!" the woman shrieked.

The commotion brought the manager out from behind the counter. "What's the problem, Ma'am?"

"This fool's making a mess all over again," the woman complained. "He got soda all over my son." She pointed at her son's pants, which were practically soaked with soda from spilling the super-size cup in the first place.

"You did that?" the bewildered manager asked Lightbulb.

"No, sir." Lightbulb stammered.

"You calling me a liar?" the woman hollered.

"No, ma'am, I'm sure he's just mistaken," the man-

6 **to swipe:** wischen 9 **to shriek:** kreischen

ager quickly said. "I'll be glad to replace any food that was spoiled. Why don't you take a seat over here?" He showed her to an empty table, then said to Lightbulb, "As soon as you finish cleaning up this mess, I want to see you in the back."

Lightbulb hung his head like a scolded puppy. He finished wiping and mopping and went in the back. By now it was our turn to order and I got a big bucket of chicken with some sides of mashed potatoes. Terrell got a meal to go and paid for everything. We headed back toward Douglass.

"Guess you could always get a job at King Chicken," Terrell said with a chuckle.

6 **scolded:** gescholten

Twenty-seven

Back home, I was the big hero. Gramma, Nia and I sat around the TV and dug in hungrily while the twins played on the floor. The funny thing was, the three of us couldn't finish that one bucket of chicken. I guess that's how much our stomachs had shrunk from hunger.

After dinner I headed upstairs. As I climbed, I thought about Lightbulb being yelled at in King Chicken. I thought about Tanisha and that smelly mattress we had to share in that drafty, cold building. I thought about all the stuff Terrell could afford. And I thought about the first time I was climbing up these stairs. Just after Darnell died.

The people who sat around tables on TV, wearing suits and talking cracker English might say there was a choice.

20 **cracker:** gepflegt

The teachers who came for two years with Teach For Equality, and then disappeared forever, might want to think there was a choice.

The politicians looking for excuses to get on TV might want people to believe they were going to give folks like us a choice.

But everyone knew the truth: There was no choice.

Not when the only world you knew was the projects.

Jules was sitting on the steps, the sawed-off rifle across his lap, with his chin on his hand, looking bored. "What do you want?"

"Marcus here?" I asked.

"He's busy," Jules said.

"Tell him it's Kalon."

One of Jules's eyebrows went up, the other went down. "So?"

"You don't tell him, I will." I started to go around him. Jules sprang to his feet and aimed the rifle at me. I stopped, but I didn't feel scared. I was sick of people aiming guns at me. I was so sick of this damned creepy life here.

9 **rifle:** Gewehr 10 **lap:** Schoß 20 **creepy:** schaurig, beschissen

"You gonna shoot me?" I asked, and realized part of me almost wished he would put me out of my misery.

"I *told* you he's busy," Jules said.

"And I'm telling *you* I don't care," I said and continued past him.

"Don't." Jules kept the gun trained on me.

"I saved your sorry ass twice," I said, and kept going. "You ain't shootin' me."

Jules followed. "You don't know what you're doing. Marcus is gonna kill you for going up there. And he's gonna kill me for letting you."

Music was coming from inside Marcus's apartment. I rapped my knuckles hard against the door. Jules hung back as if to stay clear of whatever mayhem was about to come.

I knocked again. This time harder and longer. I heard a door bang inside, and then the thud of footsteps across a floor. "Who's there?" Marcus's voice was loud and annoyed.

"Kalon."

There was a moment of silence, then bolts on the

2 **put s.o. out of their misery:** jmd. von seinem Unglück erlösen
7 **to save s.o.'s ass:** jmd. aus Schwierigkeiten befreien
14 **mayhem:** Chaos, Aufruhr

other side of the door clinked. Out of the corner of my eye, I saw Jules take another step back.

The door swung open and Marcus stood there bare chested with bare feet and his big black gun in his hand. It looked like he'd taken just enough time to pull on a pair of pants, but not enough time to buckle the belt. Behind him a woman wrapped in a white sheet stood in the bedroom doorway. Marcus scowled at me, then turned and glowered at Jules.

"I tried to stop him," Jules stammered. "I swear."

"He did," I said. "But I told him he'd have to shoot me."

Marcus's thick eyebrows dipped. He told Jules to go back to his post. I waited until he was all focused on me again before I took the white envelope out of my jacket. With a frown, Marcus slid the gun into his waistband. "What's this?"

"The bail money. You said it couldn't be kept by a Disciple."

He blinked, almost as if he'd forgotten about it. "Never told a soul, did you?"

7 **sheet:** Bettlaken 9 **to glower:** finster ansehen
16 **waistband:** Hosenbund

"No, sir."

"You sure you want to do this?"

"Yeah." I held it out for him to take.

"Keep it."

"But –"

A crooked, knowing smile broke through his lips. "Open it."

I did as I was told. Except for the $50 and $100 he'd shown me the day he gave it to me, the rest of the bills were all $1s. It took me a moment to understand. It had been a test.

"Stay here," Marcus said, and went away. He came back a moment later. "Turn around."

I did as I was told and felt a string of beads go around my neck. Marcus tied them in the back. It reminded me of the day of Darnell's funeral when he'd tied my tie. "Come back in an hour and we'll talk."

Back in our apartment, Gramma and Nia were watching TV. My sister had the twins beside her, both sucking hungrily at bottles of sugar water. I gestured for her to

6 **crooked:** schief

join me in the kitchen and gave her the $100 bill from the envelope.

Nia's eyes widened. "Where'd you get this?"

I pulled down the neck of my T-shirt and showed her the beads.

SIXTEEN YEARS OLD

Young unemployed black men murder each other at nine times the rate of white youths.

Twenty-eight

Tanisha and I continued to see each other. William had moved in with a girlfriend and Tanisha hardly saw him anymore. At my place the twins were crawling now and the apartment felt even smaller and more cramped than before.

None of the promises the politicians had made on TV had come true. I heard somewhere that the 10- and 9-year-old shooters had been charged with murder and were being held in juvie.

Laqueta had died from an overdose.

Darius, the most talented wannabe rapper in the projects, got himself arrested for armed robbery.

Precious and Imani both had babies, but now Terrell was hanging around a girl named Ambrosia.

17 **wannabe:** Möchtegern

Marcus kept me close. He had me sit in on meetings with Jamar and other high-level gang members while street level souljas and dealers older than me were kept out. My job was to keep quiet and listen.

"How much?" Marcus asked one night in his apartment when Jamar brought in a gun dealer who had three AK-47s to sell. The dealer, Jamar and Marcus were sitting in the deep, black leather chairs in front of his flat screen TV. A basketball game was on, the sound muted. I sat in a corner, playing Underground Racer on my cell phone.

"Twelve hundred a piece," said the dealer. "But I'll hook you up with all three for three Gs flat."

Marcus rubbed his chin. "Sounds high to me."

"It's a good deal," Jamar said.

"These guns got a Hellfire switch to turn 'em automatic," Jamar said. "You can empty a fifty clip in five seconds. Nobody gonna mess with that kind of firepower. Nobody."

"I'll think about it," Marcus said.

From my seat in the corner, I glanced up, curious to

7 **AK-47:** sowjet-russisches Sturmgewehr 9 **to mute:** unterdrücken, stumm schalten 13 **G:** Abk. für "grand" = 1000 17 **clip:** Magazin

see how Jamar would take that reply. I expected that he'd be looking at Marcus or the dealer or the TV screen. But he wasn't. He was staring at me with a frown on his face. I looked back down at my cell phone.

Jamar told the dealer to go out into the hall and wait. He closed the door and returned to the couch and Marcus. "We don't buy those guns, you know who will," he whispered urgently. "The Gentry boys get ahold of those things, they'll walk right over us."

Marcus nodded gravely.

"So?" Jamar sounded impatient.

"Go out in the hall and give me a minute," Marcus said.

"What?" Jamar looked surprised.

"You heard me."

I kept my eyes on my cell phone, but I had a feeling that if I'd looked up, it would have been into Jamar's eyes.

Marcus let Jamar out, then picked up the clicker and turned up the sound. The roar of the basketball crowd filled the room while he went into the kitchen. Return-

8 **to get ahold of sth.:** etw. in die Hände bekommen
9 **to walk right over s.o.:** (ugs.) jmd. völlig überlegen sein

ing with two beers, he gestured for me to join him in front of the TV. "What do you think?" he asked in a low voice.

I twisted the top off my beer and took a drink. "I'm thinkin' maybe that dealer has more than three AKs. Maybe he has six."

Marcus folded his hands together as if in prayer and tapped the knuckles against his chin. "If we don't buy three, what stops him from sellin' all six to the Gangstas?"

"He sells six to the Gangstas, those'll be the last guns he sells around here for a long time," I said.

Marcus kept tapping. "So you think the only way he can keep sellin' guns is if he keeps the sides even? And I think maybe you're right, but what if you're wrong?"

I had an idea and leaned close, whispering.

A few moments later, when Marcus invited Jamar and the dealer back into the apartment, I was once again sitting in the corner, playing with my cell phone.

"I want six," Marcus said.

"And I'm willin' to pay fifteen hundred each."

Seeing big dollar signs, the dealer took the bait. "I might be able to get three more."

"You *sure*?" Jamar challenged him with obvious disapproval.

The dealer hesitated, as if sensing he'd made a mistake. "Well, uh ..."

"Nine Gs for the six," Marcus said.

The dealer's eyes darted at Jamar, who stared back coldly at him. But the lure of an easy $9,000 was too much. "Half now, half on delivery?"

Marcus got up and went into the bedroom. A few moments later he came back and I heard the slither of bills being counted.

Thanks to the Disciples, I had money now. Enough to pay the rent on time and make sure the twins had Pampers and baby food. Gramma had gotten over the shingles, but instead of going back to cleaning houses, she took care of the twins. Nia went to school once in a while, but she spent most of her time with Tyrone, her

13 **slither:** Rutschen, schleifendes Geräusch

new boyfriend. When he wasn't gangbanging, Tyrone was scratching out lyrics – another wannabe rap star.

On Saturday nights Tanisha and I would take separate buses and meet downtown to have dinner and go to clubs.

"What's wrong?" I asked at dinner one night when she was being quiet. We were sitting in a dark red leather booth at the back of an Italian restaurant. A candle flickered on the table between us.

She glanced down at the plate before her. In the candlelight her skin glowed warmly and her hair had a sheen. To me she was the most beautiful girl in the world.

"Come on, Tani, tell me."

Her eyes met mine. "William knows something's going on. All of a sudden he's coming around more. And calling at strange times. If I get home late from school, he wants to know where I've been. If I say I'm going babysitting, he wants to know for who. I'm scared, Kalon."

"Of what?" I reached across the table and took her hand.

"You know."

"That he'll come after me?"

"That he'll *kill* you," Tanisha said in a low voice. "You heard him say so yourself."

"That's what he has to say."

Tanisha leaned forward and cupped my hand with both hers. Her face took on an urgent expression. "It's what he'd have to *do*, Kalon. The Gangstas would insist on it."

That was true. It was unacceptable to have a sister dating the enemy. Especially when you were as high up in the organization as William. It was the only way he could prove his loyalty. But I didn't want Tanisha to worry. "I can take care of myself."

Her eyes grew glittery. "If anything happened to you …"

I squeezed her hands in mine. "Nothing's gonna happen."

"You don't know."

"I never take the same route two days in a row," I said. "I hardly ever leave Frederick Douglass except to see you."

Tanisha pressed her lips together hard. "Couldn't we go away?"

That caught me by surprise. "You mean, take a trip?"

"No, I mean, for good. Someplace where there's no gangs."

"Where?" I asked.

"I don't know. Don't you have any relatives anywhere?"

All the relatives I had were right in Frederick Douglass. The only life I'd ever known was Frederick Douglass. I couldn't imagine leaving Gramma and Nia and my friends and going off to some strange place.

"We'll be okay," I said, trying to reassure her. "I promise."

After dinner we went to the Cheeta Club.

The Cheeta was loud and dark except for the flashing lights that burst on and off. I led Tanisha to the bar.

"What do you feel like?" I asked.

"Ginger ale."

"That's all?" Usually she had a seven and seven or a

21 **seven and seven:** Mischung aus Seagrams 7 Whisky und 7-UP

rum and Coke. "Come on, loosen up. This is the only night of the week we get to have fun. Nothing bad's gonna happen."

We danced until it was time to go, then stood in a dark doorway near the bus stop and kissed. It was late and the streets were empty. The night air was warm and a few of the brighter stars were visible in the dark sky. When the bus's headlights appeared several blocks away, our kisses grew more passionate.

"I love you," she whispered. It was the first time.

"I love you," I whispered back.

The driver looked at us impatiently. Tanisha climbed on and took the closest seat to the bus driver. The doors closed. Tanisha waved through the window.

I was alone in the dark at the bus stop. I always made sure she got on her bus first. Fortunately it stopped right in front of her building so she didn't have a long walk in the dark when she got back to Gentry. A siren wailed in the distance and some car horns honked. Tanisha was right. We couldn't keep going this way. Sooner or later the wrong people were going to find out.

A dozen yards away, a car pulled up to the corner, its headlights illuminating a graffiti-covered store gate across the street. It sat there for a moment. A cab came down the street and passed, then an old man with a scruffy beard rode by on a rickety old bike singing to himself.

It grew quiet again. The car at the corner hadn't moved. The engine was running and the lights were still on. Then the window came down. I could see the silhouette of someone inside. My heart began to bang and rattle. A faint glimmer of something metallic appeared.

I dove.

Pow! Zing! Ping! It was too loud to be a handgun or a rifle. Only a shotgun made a burst like that.

Screech! Tires screamed as the car tore around the corner and came down the block toward me.

I jumped to my feet and thought for an instant about running, but the car would beat me wherever I was going. Instead I stood sideways behind a lamp post and pulled my gun, a 10-shot Tec .38.

Pow! Whizz! Clink! Clank! Clang! The second shot-

5 **rickety:** wackelig 12 **to dive:** sich auf den Boden werfen
14 **shotgun:** Schrotflinte 15 **to tear:** rasen

gun blast was a flash of light and more buckshot zinged past my head. Pellets ricocheted off the lamppost. I raised the Tec, hands locked together, arms sweeping with the movement of the car, my heart banging almost as hard as the gunshots themselves. *Bang! Bang! Bang!* I fired three shots. A rear side window shattered. The car skidded sideways out of control, fishtailed left and right, then came to a stop in the middle of the street. I stayed behind the lamppost, trying to hold my gun steady despite my shaking hands and thudding heart.

Someone moved inside the car, but it was too dark to see. The windshield wipers went on and then off, as if someone had pushed the wrong lever. Then the car started to move again. This time, away down the street.

1 **buckshot:** Schrotkugeln 7 **to fishtail:** hin und her schleudern

Twenty-nine

I spent the rest of the night curled up on the grimy floor under a staircase in some building. Couldn't chance going back out into the dark. The shooters in that car might have come back. I kept thinking about the way Tanisha had acted at dinner. How worried and scared she'd been. Almost like she knew something bad might happen.

By the time the lobby began to fill with natural light, footsteps were coming down the stairs. There were the heavy thumps of men going to work, and the lighter steps of mothers and taps of children. This wasn't the projects. It was a part of town where people had regular jobs and schedules. Where men came home at night, and kids went to school until high school was over.

When there were a lot of people on the sidewalk out-

9 **to chance:** riskieren

side, I crawled out from under the staircase. One of my pants' knees was torn. The palms of my hands were scraped from diving to the ground.

I tucked in my shirt and was sliding my gun into my waistband holster when the door to one of the ground floor apartments opened. A woman came out with two little kids. The kids were dressed in clean clothes and carrying backpacks for school. The woman gasped when she saw the gun, then protectively reached for her kids and drew them back.

"It's okay," I said. "I'm going."

Holding the kids close, the woman frowned and her mouth began to move. "You're … you're just a boy."

I don't know what I expected her to say, but it wasn't that. Maybe it was true. People said I looked young for my age, but it had been a long time since I'd felt like "just a boy."

"Goddamn Jamar," Marcus muttered as we sat in his car the next evening. "I told him I wanted him for this."

I didn't ask where we were going. Marcus would tell

9 **protectively:** schützend

me when the time was right. The evening was damp and slightly chilly. Wet spring mist hung in the air and covered everything, making street lamps glitter and cars look dull. Marcus drove past the rail yards and into a part of town where I'd never been before. It was mostly old, brick factory buildings with broken windows and boarded-up doors.

Marcus stopped the car beside an empty lot. I looked out at the rubble and mounds of garbage bags that had been discarded there. Poking out of the pile was a red pedal car like the one I used to drive around the apartment when I was little.

He took out his phone and tried a number again. It rang until the message came on. He snapped the phone shut, then propped an elbow against the steering wheel, made a fist and pressed it against his forehead. His eyes were closed and I knew he was thinking hard, searching for a solution to whatever problem had beset him. For the first time ever I sensed he was scared of whatever it was he had to do next. Finally he took his fist from his forehead and opened his eyes.

2 **chilly:** kühl   4 **dull:** stumpf, glanzlos   9 **rubble:** Schutt
10 **to discard:** wegwerfen   11 **pedal car:** Tretauto
18 **to beset:** plagen, heimsuchen

"Got your gun?" he asked, staring out into the dark.

"Yeah, but –"

"But what?"

"I had to use it last night and I ain't reloaded."

"Use it how?"

"Someone took a shot at me."

Marcus frowned and looked at me. "Who?"

"Don't know. It was dark. They were in a car."

"You shot back? Think you hit anyone?"

"Might have," I said.

Marcus reached across to the glove compartment, pulled out a steel gun with a tan grip and handed it to me. It was a .44 caliber.

"Get in the back and stay down."

I did as I was told and Marcus started to drive again. "We're gonna pick up those AK-47s. You stay in the car. Anything goes wrong, you know what to do."

I crouched down in the space between the seats, staying low, squeezing the .44. The grip slowly grew warm in my hand. The car turned and bounced slightly as if going into a driveway. It stopped and Marcus got out. I

12 **tan:** hellbraun

stayed low and listened. There were voices. Someone asked Marcus if he'd come alone and he answered yes. Then someone else spoke. It sounded like Jamar. I raised my head and peeked around the headrest. It was dark and we were in a parking lot behind some buildings. Marcus was talking to Jamar and the gun dealer. There was something strange about Jamar and at first I couldn't tell what it was. Then I realized from the way his jacket was draped over his shoulders that his arm must have been in a sling. I couldn't hear what they were saying, but maybe it didn't matter.

Crouched behind the car seat, I relaxed and yawned.

Pop!

The sound of the shot made me jump. My first impulse was to look up and see what had happened. But something told me not to. If it was Jamar and Marcus and the gun dealer, then it had to be the dealer who got it, right? But I wasn't sure, so I stayed low in the back of Marcus's car and waited. A shoe scraped against the asphalt. I slowly lifted my head and peeked. Jamar and the gun dealer were walking toward Jamar's black Escalade

21 **Escalade:** Cadillac-SUV

on the other side of the parking lot. I stretched up just a hair more and caught my breath.

Marcus lay on the asphalt.

"If anything goes wrong," he'd said. *"You know what to do."*

What did that mean? If Jamar had killed Marcus, I knew what to do. *But not now. Not here*. Not when it was two against one. And not before I knew why and what was going on. So I stayed low and waited until I heard the Escalade leave, then got out of the car. Marcus lay face down on the wet asphalt, a small hole in the back of his head and a spreading puddle of blood on the ground.

Light mist floated down in the dark. I could feel it seeping into my hair. Why had they killed Marcus?

Thirty

Staying in the misty shadows, I walked the dark side streets home. There was no telling who might see me if I walked down Abernathy Avenue. By the time I got back to Frederick Douglass the mist had soaked my hair. I was crossing the yard when my cell phone rang. It was Jamar. "Where are you?"

"In the lobby," I answered.

"Come up."

"What's up?" I pretended not to know.

"Something happened to Marcus," he said.

I slid my hand inside my jacket and felt the .44. There was always a chance Jamar wanted me dead, too. There was a chance he was the one who'd tried to kill me at the bus stop.

I went upstairs slowly and carefully, stopping and checking before going around each corner. By the time I got to the fifteenth floor, most of the Disciples were already there, talking in hushed voices and looking agitated. Terrell came over to me.

"They got Marcus," he whispered. "We're squaddin' up. This is war. Jamar got some AKs. We're gonna mess them up good."

"*Who* got Marcus?" I asked.

"Who do you think?"

All around the room, gangbangers were talking war. Then Jamar strutted in, his arm in a black sling.

"We going to war, right?" said Jules.

"Shut it and listen up," Jamar barked. "We ain't goin' to war. Least not right now. Marcus got shot by some crazy hype."

"You whack?" said Terrell. "Everybody knows Marcus. Ain't no hype anywhere would touch him."

"Look, I'm tellin' you it was some hype," Jamar insisted. "Marcus got soft. He lost respect. It ain't the same as it used to be."

7 **to mess s.o. up:** jmd. fertig machen 12 **to strut:** stolzieren

"So what're we gonna do?" Bublz asked, nervously chewing a fingernail.

"Nothin'," Jamar said.

A puzzled hush settled over the group.

"Only now you're in charge?" I asked.

Jamar locked eyes with me, then looked around the room. "Anyone got a problem with that?"

The other Disciples averted their eyes and shook their heads silently.

"All right," said Jamar. "Then it's back to business as usual. Nothing changes. Only I give the orders from now on."

Terrell and I started down the stairs. I waited until we were almost to the sixth floor and then stopped him.

"Listen up," I said in a low voice. "I gotta tell you something, and you gotta swear not to tell anyone else, understand? It's the most serious thing I'm ever gonna tell you and if you tell a soul, it'll probably get me killed."

He nodded and gave me a curious look.

8 **to avert:** abwenden

"You were right before," I said. "Marcus wasn't killed by a hype. You and I know damn well that if some hype did it, the first thing Jamar would do was have him killed."

Terrell's eyebrows jumped as he realized this was true. "Then who …?"

"Jamar."

Terrell's jaw fell open and his forehead wrinkled. "But –"

I held up my hand to stop him. "I was there. It was an ambush. Jamar doesn't know I saw him."

"Why?" Terrell asked.

"Why do you think?"

My friend's face went stony. "You don't want to tell the others?"

"They won't believe me," I answered. "Or some will and some won't and then we'll have a war among ourselves."

"Folks know you don't lie."

I shook my head. "This is too big. They won't know what to believe. They might think I'm trying to take over. That after Jamar I'd be next in line. Besides, if anyone tells Jamar, he'll have me killed for sure."

Terrell's eyes wrinkled slightly. "Why you telling me?"

"If anything happens to me, I need you to know why, and do what's right," I said.

Thirty-one

The next morning I got up early and went out unarmed for the first time in months. It was too soon for the funeral notices for Marcus to start going up in the stairwells. I walked to Munson High.

"Kalon, what an unexpected surprise." Mr. White, the fat, bald principal greeted me. "What brings you to school today?"

There was no point in lying. It was the first time I'd been to school in two weeks. "Just want to see my girl, Mr. White."

"At least you're honest," Mr. White said. "Why don't you go straight to my office and wait for me there."

I did as I was told. He showed up about twenty minutes later, sat down and typed on the computer. "Let's see. Ah, here we are. In the past two months you've missed twenty-seven days of school. Not exactly a stellar attendance record, is it?"

I didn't answer. I'd already told him why I was there.

Mr. White scratched the side of his face. "School's not supposed to be a place where we come just to socialize, De Shawn. And you can't learn very much when your attendance averages one day a week."

I nodded.

"Do you have a job?" he asked.

"Not really, sir."

"May I ask what you do with your free time?"

We both knew exactly what I did.

Mr. White picked up a pencil and tapped the top of his desk. "You're from Douglass?"

"Yes, sir."

"There's a boy in your grade from over there. Extraordinarily bright."

"Lightbulb."

"Sorry?"

"Raydale," I said. "Raydale Diggs."

2 **stellar:** großartig, brilliant 3 **attendance record:** Anwesenheitsnachweis 6 **to socialize:** unter Leute gehen, sich mit Freunden treffen

"You know him?"

"He's workin' at King Chicken," I said. Lightbulb had worked his way up to the counter. He knew the price of every item by heart, and no matter how complicated the order, he automatically added it up in his head, and calculated the tax and change.

Mr. White shook his head sadly. "So much wasted potential. They talk about inner-city crime. But the real crime is what happens to boys like him and you." He glanced at the computer and back at me. "You're not here to make any trouble?"

"No, sir."

"I trust you, Kalon. And if you ever decide you really want to come back to school in a serious way, I can help you."

"Thank you, sir."

"Get your brother to arrange a meeting between me and Rance," I said. Tanisha and I were standing in a doorway outside the cafeteria. It was raining, but as long as we stood close to the doors, we wouldn't get wet.

6 **tax:** Steuer; in den USA werden Preise grundsätzlich nur netto angegeben, Mehrwert- und Verkaufssteuer wird erst an der Kasse dazugerechnet

"Are you crazy?" Tanisha said, hugging herself for warmth.

"Serious as I can be."

"He'll kill you."

"Maybe not."

"Maybe definitely."

"It's important, Tani."

"Not as important as you stayin' alive."

"Tell him we gotta meet somewhere neutral."

"He won't do it."

"Tanisha, you gotta *make* him do it."

"I can't."

I moved close and put my hands on her hips, holding her steady and looking into her eyes.

"Tani, you ever want the day to come when you and me can be together?"

Her eyes began to glitter. "We can't be together if you're dead," she sniffed.

"We can't be together while I'm alive either," I said. "Unless you help me."

I was walking home when I became aware of a car slowly moving along Abernathy. It was a dark green Crown Victoria, a favorite among undercover cops. In a way that was good news, and I relaxed. It was unlikely that a cop wanted to take a shot at me.

The window went down. "Hey, Kalon." It was Officer Patterson. "Congratulate me. I made detective."

I kept walking. He had to be crazy to think I'd stop and speak to him. If anyone saw me, I was a dead man.

"Looks like we're both rising in our respective organizations," Patterson continued.

At the corner I stopped and waited for traffic to pass. But I didn't look at him.

While the Crown Vic slowly pulled away, I heard Patterson's clear sharp voice: "Meet me under the bridge into the rail yard in twenty minutes. We need to talk."

To get to the bridge, I had to take a roundabout route through abandoned buildings and over backyard fences to make sure I wasn't followed. Patterson was standing in the shadows alone. No sign of the Crown Vic or anyone else. I walked in and stopped half a dozen yards

2 **Crown Victoria:** Ford-Limousine 3 **cop:** (ugs.) Bulle
10 **respective:** jeweilig 17 **roundabout:** umständlich, verschlungen

away from him. Water dripped from the bridge into puddles and I thought I heard the scratching and scampering of rats in the dark corners. Even homeless people wouldn't sleep there.

"I won't keep you long," Patterson said. "I know what would happen if any of your crew found out. No one's coming."

I looked around, uncomfortably.

"You're taking a chance, too," I replied.

Patterson smiled. "You never struck me as a cop killer, Kalon. Just another lost kid who's run out of options. How old are you?"

"Sixteen."

"How old do you think Marcus Elliot was?"

"Twenty-seven? Twenty-eight?"

"Try twenty. He would have turned twenty-one next month."

The news surprised me, just as Patterson knew it would.

"It's all about the pose," Patterson said. "Marcus learned how to put on impressions pretty early. For him

2 **puddle:** Pfütze 20 **pose:** Pose, Attitüde
21 **to put on impressions:** einen Eindruck erwecken

it was the only way." He paused, then continued. "But I guess you know that's not what I want to talk about. You know that Jamar's playing both sides against the middle? Making a fortune selling guns and ammo to the Disciples and the Gangstas."

I'd known that for a long time. "How come you don't bust him?"

"Certain people ... people a lot more cynical than me, seem to think that we're better off letting gangbangers kill each other. It's a lot cheaper than putting them in jail, and it only becomes a problem when things get out of hand."

"Like when shorties shoot pregnant mothers," I said.

He nodded sadly. "Or innocent bystanders get caught in the crossfire."

"Like my mother."

"Yes, Kalon. Mothers, little kids, the kind of stuff that makes the news. And then people have to pretend they're outraged and they're gonna do something about it until something else comes along and grabs the head-

3 **to play both sides against the middle:** zwei Seiten gegeneinander ausspielen 4 **ammo:** (kurz für "ammunition") Munition
7 **to bust s.o.:** jmd. hochnehmen, verhaften
15 **bystander:** Passant, Unbeteiligter 20 **outraged:** empört

lines. People have short attention spans. All it takes is a hurricane or a bridge collapse to make them forget. Especially when it comes to the projects. All these young girls with two or three children by different fathers. All these fatherless boys running around wild killing each other. People think it's a shame, but no one really knows how to fix it. So they'd just as soon pretend it doesn't exist."

"If you believe that, why'd you bother becoming a cop?" I asked.

"So I can fall asleep at night knowing that while I can't fix it, at least I'm on the right side. How you sleeping these days, Kalon?"

I looked around again, letting Patterson know that I was ready to go.

"We could work together," Patterson said. "No one would ever know. You could help me take down Rance Jones and his top lieutenants. Then we'd go after Jamar. You'd be arrested on some fake charge so it wouldn't look like you were the snitch. When the time is right, we could move you, your gramma, sister and those kids

19 **charge:** Beschuldigung, Verdacht

someplace new. Someplace where you could get a fresh start."

"That's what you're offering me? A fresh start?"

Patterson nodded. "Marcus Elliott didn't live to be twenty-one. You're sixteen, Kalon. How long you think you're gonna last?"

Thirty-two

Two days later my cell phone rang and a voice said, "Two am tonight. The parking lot behind King Chicken. Come alone and unarmed. And don't wear no colors."

I did as I was told. It was a cool night and I wore jeans, a shirt, and a sweater so it would be easier to see that I wasn't carrying. When I got there, the parking lot was empty. The moon was almost full. The smell of fried chicken was in the air. I stood in the middle of the lot with my hands hanging loose at my side.

A broad-shouldered figure walked slowly around the side of the building, casting a moon-lit shadow, looking quickly to the left and right. William. He took out a gun. Even in the dark I could tell that it was a Glock.

10 **colors:** Gangabzeichen 14 **to carry:** (ugs.) bewaffnet sein

"Turn around and put your hands against the wall," he said.

I faced the wall and felt the hard end of the gun barrel poke the small of my back. With his free hand William patted me down.

"You alone?"

"Yeah."

He stepped close to my right side, poking the Glock into my ribs. "I ought to shoot you right now," he muttered in a low voice. "What do you think you're doing? Trying to get us all killed?"

"No."

"Then you must be stupid," he snarled. "Seeing my sister, sending word you want to see Rance. What do you think he's gonna do to me when he figures out what's going on? What do you think he's gonna do to my sister?"

We'd find out soon enough. A black Range Rover pulled into the lot. The windows were as dark as its body and it had big shiny rims. Still facing the wall, I looked over my shoulder and saw Big D get out of the

5 **to pat s.o. down:** jmd. abtasten

car. I remembered him from the day they almost shot Snoop.

"Keep your hands against the wall," he said, and slid his hands up and down my arms and legs and around my torso, just as William's had a few moments before. These guys weren't taking any chances. When he finished he clamped a meaty hand on my shoulder and spun me around. He was holding a gun.

"You, me, and William gonna get in that car," he said. "You try anything funny, I'll blow a hole right through your spine."

I started toward the car. William walked ahead, and Big D behind. I knew the gun aimed right at my spine. When we got to the car, I reached toward the rear door.

"No." Big D poked me in the back. "In the front. Passenger side."

I did as I was told and got into the front passenger seat. William got into the driver's seat and held the Glock low in his lap, aimed at me. The temptation to turn around and look at Rance was great, but I controlled myself.

11 **spine:** Rückgrat

Then I smelled something sweet and flowery.

"What the ...?" William smelled it, too, and turned around.

I didn't have to look to know that they had Tanisha in the back seat. My stomach started to knot.

"Turn around," a voice said.

I turned. Tanisha was squeezed between Big D and Rance Jones. Rance had grown a goatee beard since I'd last seen him. Tanisha was wincing and I could see why: Rance was pressing the barrel of a gun into her ribs.

"Now turn back around so I don't have to look at your ugly Disciple face again," Rance grunted.

I did as I was told. My eyes met William's. His were filled with rage.

"Talk," Rance said.

"Why'd you have Jamar kill Marcus?" I asked.

A slight gasp came from the back seat, and I suspected that Rance had jabbed the gun harder into Tanisha's ribs. "Who else knows?" he asked. "And tell the truth or she dies."

I heard a click and knew Rance had cocked the gun.

5 **to knot:** sich verkrampfen 8 **goatee beard:** Ziegenbart
21 **to cock a gun:** eine Waffe spannen

A pulse in my forehead throbbed painfully. Every muscle in my body was tense. I heard a sniff and a brief sob as if Tanisha was trying to fight back tears. But I had to believe Rance wouldn't shoot her. Not with William there. It had to be a bluff.

"You kill her and I'll tell the Disciples about Jamar," I said. "You kill me, my friend will tell."

I didn't think a shot would follow, but if it did, I would grab William's gun and kill Rance, or die trying. Because I wouldn't want to live knowing I was responsible for Tanisha's death.

But the shot didn't come. At least, not yet.

"Maybe I don't believe you," Rance said. "Give me one good reason why I shouldn't kill you right now."

"You think you're playing Jamar," I said, "but it's the other way around. He's playing you."

There was an uncomfortable silence. In the front seat beside me William cast an uncertain glance back.

"Keep talkin'," Rance ordered.

"Did he and that gun dealer friend of his try to get you to buy three AK-47s?"

3 **sob:** Schluchzen

"How …" Rance started to ask, then caught himself. "So what?"

"They had six," I said. "Jamar wanted to make sure Douglass got the other three."

Silence again. Then Rance's voice. "That doesn't matter."

"How can it not matter?" I asked back. "He's gonna keep selling you and the Disciples ammo and guns and let you keep shooting at each other forever."

"No, he ain't," Rance said. "'cause there ain't gonna be two gangs much longer."

"Jamar know that?"

"He will when I want him to," Rance said.

"What makes you think you can trust him?"

"He's proved himself."

"By ambushing Marcus?" I wanted to know more. "What did he have to lose? Now he thinks that he's the boss."

"He's done worse."

Denzel, I thought. "Behind the hobby center?"

"That and worse," said Rance.

Worse than killing Denzel? I tried to think. Then I remembered Darnell. "That's why he threw that shorty out the window?"

"Not just any shorty," Rance replied. "Marcus's nephew. See? He'll do anything I say. And that's all he gotta do. Now that Marcus is gone, there's just gonna be one gang around here. Mine."

I took a deep breath and chose my next words carefully. "There's one thing you need that Jamar can't deliver."

"Oh, yeah? What's that?" Rance sounded amused.

"Loyalty," I said.

Another silence. Then Rance took up my cue. "Well, that might just be because there's a rotten apple in the barrel."

I felt the gun against the back of my head. *Click!* Rance cocked the trigger. "Get out."

I was trembling from head to foot and felt light-headed like I was going to be sick. Rance had every reason to kill me. This was the end.

"Get him out," Rance snapped.

William reached across me and pushed open the door. "Out, punk."

"You can't!" Tanisha gasped.

"I got his baby," Tanisha whispered.

Everything stopped. William twisted around in his seat and stared at his sister. I felt the pressure of the gun barrel slowly ease from the back of my skull.

She stared back at me with eyes glittery with tears. "It's true."

"Ha!" Rance laughed harshly. "Surprise, surprise."

"How come you didn't tell me, Tani?" My voice was shaking.

"I was going to," Tanisha said with a sniff. William cursed under his breath.

"I don't think you know how lucky you just got, punk," Rance said.

Rance aimed his gun at my face. "You get one chance to prove your loyalty. Mess up and you won't get another, understand?"

I nodded.

Rance gestured at the open car door. "Go home and

7 **to ease:** nachlassen

don't say nothin' to no one. The Disciples are gonna find out soon enough anyway. You do what you're told and you and your girl and that little baby'll be okay."

I walked home under the moonlight, thinking about Tanisha. *Now what?* I wasn't like Terrell. I couldn't abandon the mother of my child. And that meant there would soon be two more mouths in our family to feed. My fate was sealed.

Ahead, the red and blue lights of police cars flashed. As I got closer to Douglass I saw a crowd and bright beams of light sweeping the ground in front of my building. A dozen police officers had cordoned off the area around the bench. Some were keeping people away while others flashed lights at the building. Inside the cordoned-off area were men wearing street clothes – detectives – including Patterson.

Lightbulb was leaning against a tree, wearing blue coveralls. He'd been fired from King Chicken and now worked the night shift as a janitor, washing bathrooms in office buildings from 6 pm to 2 am.

13 **to cordon off:** absperren 20 **janitor:** Hausmeister

I stopped beside him. "What's going on?"

"Jamar got hisself shot," Lightbulb said.

I had a feeling. "You seen Terrell?"

He shook his head. We watched while they zipped Jamar into a body bag and wheeled him toward an ambulance parked on Abernathy. The police and detectives stayed bunched together, those high-powered beams sweeping around as they made their way back to their cars. One of the beams swept in my direction, temporarily blinding me. I shielded my eyes and saw a figure step toward me.

"Hey, Kalon," Patterson said. "How does that song go? Another one bites the dust. Who do you think's gonna be next?"

I didn't answer. Instead, I went inside and up to Terrell's apartment.

Terrell's momma opened the door. She looked older than ever. Even though it was past 2 am the TV was on loud.

"Terrell in trouble?" she asked in a low voice.

"No, ma'am," I said. "Is he here?"

She pointed down the hall to his room.

Terrell was sitting at his desk with his feet up and headphones on, playing Grand Theft Auto. When he saw me, he offered me a bag of peanuts. "Yo, s'up?"

I closed the door. "Why?"

"Why what?"

"You know what I'm talking about," I said. "Where's your gun?"

Terrell quickly glanced at the door. "Keep it down. My momma'll hear."

"She's gonna hear plenty soon enough anyway," I returned, lowering my voice. "Now where is it?"

"Threw it down the sewer," Terrell hissed. "You think I'd be stupid enough to keep it?"

"Why not? You were stupid enough to use it."

Terrell's face hardened. "He killed Marcus. No way he was gonna lead the Disciples. I made sure of that."

"You *tell* anyone he killed Marcus?" I asked.

Terrell shook his head. "You told me not to."

"So when *were* you gonna tell them?"

Terrell didn't answer.

"You didn't just kill Jamar because he killed Marcus," I said. "You killed him to prove to everyone that you can lead the Disciples."

Terrell gazed steadily at me. "So? What's wrong with that? It's a dog-eat-dog world, right? Besides, Jamar deserved it."

"There's just one problem," I said. "Jamar was working for Rance."

Terrell's eyes widened. "For real?"

He balled his hand into a fist. "Then he deserved it even more."

"True that," I said. "But what do you think's gonna happen when Rance finds out you killed Jamar?"

Terrell's eyes darted to the left. "But I didn't know."

"You think that'll make a difference?"

Fear surged to Terrell's face. "What am I gonna do?" he asked.

"Go away."

"You serious?"

"You stay, I can't guarantee you'll be alive this time tomorrow."

5 **dog-eat-dog:** gnadenlos, jeder gegen jeden

"Where am I gonna go?"

I nodded at the peanut bag and said, "Get packin'. You best be gone before daylight."

Thirty-three

The next afternoon I assembled what was left of the Douglass Disciples in the yard. I sat on the back of the old bench and looked at them. A couple of them were puffy faced as if they'd just gotten up.

"What's this about?" Jules asked with a yawn.

"The future," I said.

"Where's Terrell?" Bublz asked.

I shrugged. They'd hear it soon enough.

Out on Abernathy the black Land Rover pulled up to the curb. You could feel a change in the air. All over the yard it got quiet. Mothers began to pull their children away. The old folks pushed themselves up on their walkers and canes and started to hobble back toward their buildings. Just like those old cowboy movies where the

8 **to assemble:** versammeln

town folk scattered when the bad guys arrived. Even before the Land Rover's door opened, Jules was reaching into his jacket.

"Don't," I hissed.

"But they're Gentry," Bublz sputtered.

"Let's hear what they have to say."

Jules stared suspiciously at me. "How do *you* know they want to talk?"

Big D and William got out first, taking their time and looking around. Antwan got out next. It was the first time I'd seen him since middle school, but I wasn't surprised that he was a Gangsta. Finally, Rance got out. Rance had told me earlier by phone he wanted to do it outside in the daylight. So everyone could see everyone clearly.

Rance cleared his throat. "I come in peace."

"The hell you do," Jules challenged him. "After you killed Marcus and Jamar."

"I didn't kill neither of them," Rance answered calmly.

"Then you had them killed," Tyrone said.

4 **to hiss:** zischen

Rance shook his head and gestured at me. "Tell them."

It took me a while to find my voice. "Jamar killed Marcus," I said. "Terrell killed Jamar."

The Disciples looked at me uncomprehendingly.

"Jamar killed Marcus because he wanted to take over the gang," I explained. "Terrell killed Jamar in revenge."

No one said a word. Then Tyrone broke the silence. "What's this all about?"

"Joining forces," Rance said. "What's the point of us killin' each other? I need new territory and you need new leadership."

"You expect us to just start wearing Gentry Gangsta colors?" Jules asked defiantly.

"No, I propose a new organization called the Gangsta Disciples and mix colors," Rance replied. "Black and green."

Bublz bit his lip anxiously and gave the rest of us an uncertain look. "What do you think?"

"Like we have a choice," Jules grumbled and spat on the ground.

7 **revenge:** Rache

"You got a choice in who heads up your part of the organization," Rance said.

That was a smart move. There was a short silence. Then Tyrone nodded at me. "I think it should be you."

SEVENTEEN YEARS OLD

According to the National Center for Health Statistic, in 1965 24 percent of black infants were born to single mothers. By 1990 the rate had risen to 64 percent. In 2005 it was just under 70 percent.

Thirty-four

The sound of Simon crying in another room woke me. Sunlight pressed against the red and green curtains. Still half asleep, I lay tangled in the deep blue sheets and listened to my son bawl. Simon was three months old. The baby's cries were like a little bird's squawks. Sometimes I wondered what my son would be like. What he would look and act like. Everyone said he would grow up to be good-looking like his parents. If he grew up.

Picking up the heavy gold Rolex from the night table, I saw that it was 3:54 pm. As I shaved I checked myself in the mirror. Grown-up. Quite so. Back in the bedroom there was a message on my phone. Rance wanted to see me. I was to come alone. I slipped on some clothes and slid my gun into the waistband holster.

10 **tangled:** eingewickelt, verheddert 11 **to bawl:** brüllen
12 **squawk:** Krähen, Kreischen

Out in the living room Tanisha was sitting on the couch giving Simon a bottle. Even without make-up she was a beautiful girl. The TV was on and mother and son seemed transfixed by the rapidly changing colors and images.

I gave Tanisha a kiss and left.

Out in the fifteenth floor hall, I went down a few doors and into another apartment. Inside, half a dozen people were sitting at the ping pong table, wearing white masks, filling baggies with weed and vials with rock. Jules was watching over them. He gave me a nod. Everything was okay.

Bublz was sitting at the top of the steps, playing his PSP2. Now that the two gangs had joined, we didn't really need a guard, but I kept Bublz up there because there wasn't much else he was good for.

On the way downstairs I stopped in to see my family. Gramma and Nia and her new boyfriend Nathan were watching TV. Xavier and Jayda were one and a half now. Xavier was sitting on the floor, playing with some plastic blocks. He was a chubby, happy little boy with fat

4 **to transfix:** in Bann schlagen
9 **white masks:** Atemschutzmasken

thighs and a belly. Jayda was thinner and edgy. She sat next to her mother, sucking her thumb and rubbing her pink baby blanket against her face. I stroked Xavier's head and he looked up at me and grinned.

Just about everything in the apartment – the TV, the toys, the baby clothes, the food – was there because I'd paid for it.

"Yo, what up, bro?" Nathan waved from the couch. He was short and heavy-set and happy to eat the food I paid for and watch TV and play video games all day. I nodded tersely, not happy that he was freeloading off my sister. But Nia's belly was big with his baby.

Gramma looked up from the TV. "You goin' downstairs?"

"Yep."

"Get me some mint chocolate chip."

"Ain't got time."

"Don't give me that," Gramma huffed. "Just because you a big shot now. I remember changing your stinky diapers."

Nia gave me a crooked smile. I may have been a co-

1 **edgy:** nervös 11 **tersely:** knapp, kurz angebunden
to freeload off s.o.: sich von jmd. aushalten lassen
18 **to huff:** schnauben 20 **diapers:** Windeln

leader of the biggest gang in the projects now, but as far as Gramma was concerned, I was still her gopher.

Outside, the bench was empty. A kid named Arnet was supposed to be there. Feeling anger start to simmer, I spotted him over by the wall chatting up a couple of girls. By the time Arnet saw me coming it was too late. I smacked him hard on the side of the head and he stumbled and fell down. The girls backed away to a safe distance.

"I say you could leave the bench?" I asked coldly.

Sitting on the ground, his hand on the place where I'd slapped him, Arnet's eyes darted around as if searching for an escape route. "Ain't no customers."

"Maybe that's 'cause there ain't no one there to sell 'em anything," I snapped. "Get back on that bench."

He jumped to his feet and scurried back. I was about to leave when one of the girls caught my eye. She had long shiny hair, big pretty eyes, and a sexy body.

"Hi, Kalon?" she said, slinky-voiced, batting her eyes. "Know who I am?"

2 **gopher:** Botenjunge 5 **to simmer:** sieden, köcheln
6 **to chat s.o. up:** jmd. anquatschen, anmachen
20 **slinky:** aufreizend, verführerisch
to bat one's eyes/eyelids: mit den Augen klimpern

"Should I?"

"Sechelle, Lightbulb's sister."

"Lollipop?" I blinked. It was hard to believe that she was Lightbulb's sticky-faced, nappy-haired little sister.

Sechelle pursed her lips. "No one calls me that no more."

Now that I was high up in the gang, a lot of women let me know they were interested. So far I'd resisted the temptation, but it wasn't easy.

"Bet Tanisha's real busy with that new little baby," she said. "Gimme your phone."

I handed it to her and she thumbed in a number and hit save. She handed it back and smiled. "Any time."

Rance had a club in the basement of one of the Gentry buildings. It had a bar and tables and a dance floor. The year-round decorations were mostly Christmas lights and tin foil. Just about every night there was loud music and drink and drugs and thugs and loose women. Rance spent most of his time in the back room playing cards.

I parked outside the building. A couple of gangbang-

19 **thug:** Schlägertyp **loose women:** leichte Mädchen

ers were hanging around, leaning on cars. They were Gentry, and even though we were all supposed to be one big happy family now, they still gave me suspicious, uncertain looks. Especially Antwan. He blocked the entrance. "Rance expecting you?"

"That's right," I said.

"Wait here." He went inside.

The guys relaxed, but I felt their eyes on me. A moment later the door opened and Antwan waved me in. The dimly lit club smelled of stale cigarette smoke and spilled beer. A few tables were already occupied by men and women, and at the bar a couple of painted girls gave me the eye. I knocked on the door to the back room.

Big D let me in. The room was small and smoky. Rance and three other men sat around a table smoking cigars and playing cards. On the table were drinks, handguns, and poker chips. Rance swiveled his head at me. "Check him, D," he ordered.

I held out my arms. With my jacket open, the gun in my waistband was in plain sight. Big D removed it and held it up for Rance to see.

10 **stale:** alt, abgestanden; hier: kalt 12 **to give s.o. the eye:** jmd. mit Blicken anmachen

"Why'd you come in here strapped?" Rance asked while Big D patted down my legs in case I was carrying anything else.

"Same reason you did," I countered.

Rance shuffled his cards. "You planning on shooting anyone?"

"If I was, I already would have," I answered.

One of the men at the table chuckled.

"He's clean," Big D announced.

"Give me a minute," Rance said, and turned back to the table. An older man wearing a plaid golf cap won the hand and raked in a pile of chips. They filed out of the room. He pointed his finger at Big D. "You, too."

We were alone. At a small bar on the side of the room Rance reached for a bottle of Johnny Walker Blue and filled two shot glasses. "I hear William ain't happy," he said. "He seems to think I'm holding out on you and him. That what you think, too?"

"It's not for me to say," I replied.

"You unhappy with your cut?" Rance asked. "You ever imagine you'd have as much as you got now?"

11 **plaid:** kariert 12 **to rake in:** zusammenraffen
17 **to hold out on s.o.:** jmd. etw. vorenthalten 20 **cut:** Anteil

I shook my head. I'd never imagined it. Not even anything close.

"You like that crib you got? That flat screen TV and sound system? That nice BMW and all the bling? Your woman or baby wanting for anything?"

"No."

"We got a good thing here, Everyone's happy. Things are running smoothly. Nobody's shooting anymore. Why let a rotten apple spoil the barrel?" He narrowed one eye. "You know what rotten apple I'm talking about?"

"Uh huh."

"So how'd you like to make twice what you're making now?" Rance asked. "How'd you like to move out of that low life project and into a really nice crib? A place with an indoor garage for your car so you don't have to have shorties watching it on the street. A place where you can adjust the heat in the winter and have a toilet that'll flush and a bathroom with a shower. Where you don't get woken up in the middle of the night by gunfire. Nice, huh? Think how much your woman would appreciate getting set up in a place like that."

10 **rotten apple:** schwarzes Schaf   17 **to adjust:** regulieren

"That's what you have?" I'd heard he'd moved out of Gentry to another part of town.

"Absolutely," Rance said. "And you can, too. There's just one thing you gotta do."

Rance decided we'd do it that Friday. That was the day he usually met with William and me to divide up the money and take care of gang business.

It was early in the afternoon and I was just getting in my car when someone yelled, "Hey!"

I looked up. A pretty teen was hurrying toward me with a bunch of books in her arms. She looked familiar. As she got close she grinned because she could see I was puzzled.

"Come on," she said.

I took my best guess. "Precious?"

"See, it wasn't so hard," she smiled and pointed at my BMW. "That's a nice car you got, Kalon. I'm glad you're gonna give me a ride in it."

"I ain't got time."

"Oh, yes, you do," Precious said. "You gangbangers

got all the time in the world. Know why? 'cause you ain't goin' nowhere. But I am. I'm going to school and you're givin' me a ride because I'm late."

It had been a long time since anyone, except Gramma, had talked to me that way. I could have easily ignored her, or done worse. Instead, I opened the door for her.

"Since when did you start taking evening classes?" I asked as I drove toward Munson.

Precious laughed. "Since I figured out that no Prince Charming was going to come along and save my sorry ass, so I'd have to do it myself."

We rode a block in silence. Then Precious said, "Know why I knew you'd give me a ride, Kalon? You may be the top dog around here now, but inside you're different. Some of those gangbangers are bad to the bone. But not you. You never were, and you never will be. As hard as you may try."

I stopped in front of Munson. Precious jumped out and turned around. Her beaming self-confidence dumbfounded me. "Thanks for the ride. And enjoy your life, Kalon. Whatever's left of it."

9 **Prince Charming:** Märchenprinz 19 **to dumbfound s.o.:** jmd. sprachlos machen

From there I drove over to Gentry and picked up William. We were equals now. What was left of the Disciples reported to me, and the Gentry crew reported to him, and we both reported to Rance. Over the past year, he and I had gradually become more comfortable around each other. There was still some friction left over from the days when Douglass and Gentry were murderous rivals, but we were also family now. William wasn't only Tanisha's brother, he was Simon's uncle.

"Any word on how we did this week?" he asked after getting into the car.

"Guess Rance'll tell us."

"You think?" William said with a heap of sarcasm. "Suppose I told you I've been keeping track of what comes in and I know for a fact he's keeping a lot more than he's supposed to? And for what? He doesn't do nothing. Just sits in that club all day and plays cards and then goes home to that fancy crib."

"Guess he thinks he earned it," I accelerated and overtook the truck ahead of us.

"For how long?" William asked. "How long do you

6 **friction:** Spannung

want to support his lazy butt while he sits there doing nothing?"

I didn't answer. William gave me an uncertain look. "Blood's thicker than water, right? So what if something happened to Rance? Here in the 'hood things happen all the time. The cops don't care. Another gangbanger gets killed? Good riddance. With Rance gone it would be you and me. And we're blood. Tanisha needs her brother and Simon needs his father."

Kill or be killed. That's what it always came down to. Nothing to do each day but take care of business, wait for the next day to come, and wonder if you'll still be alive.

"I don't know about you," William went on, "But as far as I'm concerned, today's his last chance. Either he puts up or I'm gonna shut him up for good."

I tensed. "Not in the club."

"You think I'm stupid? He can't stay in that club forever. If things don't get right, some night I'll be waiting for him."

At the club Big D patted both of us down and took

our guns. In the back room Rance was sitting on the couch, watching baseball on TV. He glanced up at me and William.

"Is it that time of the week?" he said. It was a taunt at William. "Sorry, boys. I got five Gs on Detroit and it's the bottom of the ninth with one out left."

We waited. The Detroit batter struck out.

"Damn!" Rance muttered. He clicked off the TV. "They clean, Big D?"

"Sure are."

"Okay, you can go," said Rance without rising from the couch.

"How do we know *you're* not carrying?" William asked. It was a stupid thing to say. We'd met like this nearly every Friday for the past year and William had never said it before.

Rance slowly rose from the couch. He gestured at me and said to William, "You trust him?"

William nodded.

Rance raised his arms. "Be my guest."

I slid my hands down his body and around his legs.

4 **taunt:** spöttische Bemerkung, Stichelei 20 **be my guest:** nur zu, bitteschön

Through the pants I felt a holster strapped just above his left ankle. The gun in it was stubby with a thick grip. Probably a snub-nose .38. I glanced up at Rance and our eyes met in an instant of understanding. It was survival of the fittest. Choosing sides was always a gamble, but sometimes you had no choice. This was one of those times.

"He's clean," I lied.

Rance nodded toward the poker table. "Let's get this over with." He gestured for me to sit on his right and William on his left. Just as he did every week, he unzipped a dark green First National Bank bag and dumped the contents on the table. Out tumbled neat stacks of bills held with rubber bands. Instantly, William and I saw that there was less money on the table than previous weeks.

Without a word, Rance divided the stacks up, then leaned back in his chair and crossed his arms. "Okay, now why don't you tell me what your problem is."

"You know what my problem is." William glowered.

"You talking about how the shares work?" Rance said

2 **stubby:** kurz, gedrungen 12 **to dump:** ausschütten

as if he didn't know. "The same as they always have. Each month one third goes to me. You two split one third, and the last third goes to the rest."

"Except it seems like you're taking more than one third," said William. "There's a lot more gwap that comes in than what's on this table right now."

"That's 'cause you ain't figured in the administrative costs of running this operation," Rance replied. "There's a lot of expenses you don't see."

William nodded at the cards and poker chips on the bar. "I think I'm seeing one right now. I think you been losing a lot of our money playin' cards, and my guess is the cost of that fancy crib of yours also comes out of our share. And I'm sayin' that from now on you gotta divide the money up *before* you take out your so called administrative costs."

Rance shook his head slowly. "I don't think that's gonna happen, William."

"Kalon and I think it should."

"Is that so?" Rance gave me a feigned look of surprise.

20 **feigned:** scheinbar, vorgeblich

That was my cue. I reached under the chair where the gun was taped, pulled it out, and aimed it at William, whose jaw dropped and eyes bulged. Rance seemed pleased by the result. "See, there are certain things you don't understand, William," he said. "I worked hard to get where I am. Every gangbanger I started out with is either dead or in jail. I'm the only one left. And that means I've earned certain privileges. I'm in charge of this gang. I handle the finances. I decide what the administrative costs are. And … I decide who lives and dies."

William was trembling. "I … I thought we were blood," he stammered to me.

Rance laughed harshly. "Blood? That don't mean nothin'. Where you been, boy? This is about money and nothing else. It's about who gets what share. And too bad for you, it looks like from now on your share's going to someone else." He nodded at me. "Do it."

I slipped off the safety and looked into William's wide eyes. "Kalon," he whimpered. "How you gonna face Tanisha?"

"Don't be stupid," Rance chuckled haughtily. "Kalon's

gonna be the co-leader of the Gangsta Disciples with me. He don't have to worry about facing no one. They gonna have to worry about facing him." He looked at me again. "Now do it, boy. You want it, you gotta earn it."

Keeping the gun aimed at William, I turned my head and stared at Rance.

"You want an equal share, do it," he ordered.

I swung my arm around and aimed the gun at him. "You killed Denzel. Father of my sister's babies. Here's how I get my equal share."

Rance's eyes widened. He reached for his ankle.

I pulled the trigger.

Rance fell back and tumbled to the floor with a thud. I got up and stood behind the door as Big D burst in, gun drawn. By the time he saw Rance lying in a pool of blood, the barrel of my gun was pressed against the back of his skull. Big D raised his hands. William took the gun from him.

Antwan and some of the Gangsta raced in next with their guns drawn. I held my gun to Big D's head. "Drop 'em."

Guns clattered to the floor.

"Rance had an accident," I said calmly. "William and I are the leaders from now on. Everyone understand?"

Big D nodded slowly. The others followed his example.

"Whatever he was paying you, we'll pay you more," I said. "Big D, how's that sound to you?"

"Good," the big man said.

"You sure?" I asked.

Big D nodded at Rance's body. "Never liked that dude. He was as mean and nasty as they come."

I lowered my gun. "What kind of car do you drive, Big D?"

"Well, I ain't actually rolling right now," he said.

"How'd you like a Range Rover?" I asked.

"Serious?" Big D gasped.

I pointed at Rance's body. "I think you'll find the keys and registration on him. And take whatever cash is in his wallet and share it with these fellows."

"Yes, sir," Big D said. "Thank you, sir."

"And from now on, if anyone asks who's running this gang?" I said.

Big D knew what the answer had to be. "You two," he said, and smirked.

TWENTY-EIGHT YEARS OLD

Recent studies have shown that the huge pool of poorly educated black men are becoming ever more disconnected from the mainstream society. Especially in the country's inner cities where work is scarcer than ever and prison is routine.

scarce: selten, knapp

Prison

Four months later, a week after I turned 18, I was arrested and charged with the murder of Rance Howard, as well as with racketeering, money laundering, and drug and weapons trafficking. Before I'd killed him, Rance had made a deal with the cops, and the back room of the club had been wired for video. It was supposed to have shown me killing William. That way Rance would have gotten rid of both of us.

Instead, it showed me killing Rance. And thanks to the video, the cops didn't need the testimony of any snitches.

That was ten years ago. Today I'm sitting in a prison cell, where I will probably spend the rest of my life. Apart from the few hours we are allowed to leave our

10 **racketeering:** kriminelle Geschäftemacherei, Schutzgelderpressung **money laundering:** Geldwäsche 11 **weapons trafficking:** Waffenhandel 17 **testimony:** Zeugenaussage

cells, all I see of the world is the view through the small prison window. I will never have the opportunity to play with Simon. I will never feel the softness of Tanisha's, or any other woman's, skin against my own. I will never eat a steak, or good crispy French fries, or a milkshake again. In comparison, the projects were paradise.

According to statistics, black Americans represent 13 percent of the overall population in this country, but we make up 50 percent of the prison population. Many of these were gangstas before they came here, and here they form new gangs. Most join because they see no choice. They are afraid of what will happen if they don't. Is our situation hopeless? Sometimes it feels that way. All I know is that the only hope our people have is education. It is the only way out of poverty, and self-destruction.

I still hear from some of the people in my past. Detective Patterson's retired now. But he writes me letters now and then, mostly about what his grandchildren are up to. He's also written letters to the parole board on my behalf. But he says I shouldn't get my hopes up.

20 **parole board:** Begnadigungskommission

I hear from Nia. The twins are almost twelve, and her daughter Kalona is almost ten. They're all still in school for now, which is good. Nathan's long gone. Gramma still spends most of her days in front of the TV.

Lightbulb writes now and then. He still lives with his momma and works as a janitor. Probably will for the rest of his life. Last time he wrote he said Sechelle had some kids but they were put in foster homes because she was all messed up on drugs.

Darius got out of prison and became a recording engineer. They say he has even worked with some important rap stars.

Tanisha is a sales woman. She's married, but she sends me lots of photos and news about Simon. Precious is a registered nurse.

Just about every other guy I grew up with is either dead or in prison. But there's one other person I hear from regularly. Just this morning the guard handed me a letter from him.

10 **recording engineer:** Tontechniker

Yo Kalon,

So how they treet you up there? Ok, I hope. Things is good here. Dawn Mae is pregnant with our 3rd baby. She's really hoping for a girl now that we got 2 boys. Thomas is going into 2nd grade. Jason's in kintergarten. They are a couple of raskels.

I'm still workin my but off on the farm. After all those years being inside so much, I love being outside. Even when it's 110 and swets poorin off you like a waterfall. We put in a good crop this year and made some money. Dawn Mae says maybe it time for us to buy a house.

That detective stil trying to help you with parole? I hope so. Strange how things work out, ain't it? If someone asked me back in the day which one be married with kids and a job? And which be in jail? I'd have bet for sure it would be the other way round.

So that's all for now. Keep the faith, bro.

Terrell.

19 **to keep the faith:** sauber bleiben, zu seinen Leuten halten
bro: (kurz für "brother") Bruder, Kumpel

AFTERWORD

In my last book, *Boot Camp*, I wrote about a secret prison system for teenagers in the United States. Teens do not have to be found guilty of a crime to be sent to one of these facilities, also known as boot camps. All they have to do is be under the age of eighteen and have parents or guardians who want to send them away.

There is yet another system of detention in our country that holds not thousands, but millions, of innocent people against their wills. Unlike boot camps, which tend to be located in remote parts of the landscape, these social and economic gulags are hidden in plain sight, often in inner cities, but also anyplace where people are denied the basic social, economic, and educational opportunities necessary to succeed.

11 **facility:** Einrichtung **boot camp:** Erziehungslager
13 **guardians:** Erziehungsberechtigte 14 **detention:** Haft, Arrest
18 **gulag:** Straflager

Like many Americans, I believe that the United States provides its citizens with some of the greatest educational, social, and financial opportunities on earth. But those opportunities are not evenly shared. Our country was founded on the basis of equal rights and equal opportunity, but that no longer appears to be the case. Today significant numbers of American citizens – mostly minorities, and many living in impoverished inner-city areas – are doomed to fail before they have the chance to embrace the possibilities for a happy and rewarding life that so many of the rest of us enjoy.

For many of us who live in suburbs, small towns, and in the better parts of cities, the impoverished inner cities are portrayed by the media as a cauldron of moral decay and crime that now and then produces a talented athlete or music star. We forget that millions of inner-city denizens are just like us – well-meaning human beings who yearn for the simple and basic privileges our country promises: a decent education, a job with a chance for advancement, and a safe place to raise children.

7 **significant:** bedeutend 8 **impoverished:** verarmt
9 **doomed:** verdammt 10 **to embrace:** annehmen
rewarding: lohnend 14 **cauldron:** (Hexen-)Kessel
15 **decay:** Verfall 17 **denizen:** Bewohner
20 **advancement:** Fortkommen

Young men and women who do not enjoy these privileges try to realize their needs and dreams in a different way. Experts think this the reason why the number of gang members in the USA has risen constantly over the last three decades. Skin color and ethnicity do not play an important part in this. Up to thirty percent of the gang members are white, in particular in small towns and in the country. The majority, however, are Latino-American, Afro-American or Asian Americans.

As Malcolm W. Klein writes in his book *The American Street Gang*, there are several factors that explain the origin of street gangs: racism, poverty, minority and youth cultures, fatalism in the face of rising misery, lack of political sensitivity and the negligent indifference of most Americans who do not have to fight for survival in the ghettos.

Mankind has always joined together to improve its chance of survival. It seems to be in our nature. Maybe this human instinct explains why young men (and incidentally young women, too) see no other way to escape hopelessness, racism and poverty than to join a gang.

13 **lack of:** Mangel 14 **negligent:** nachlässig
indifference: Gleichgültigkeit

Saddest and most threatening of all, those gangs offer no positive values, alternatives or examples. Inherently good and talented teenagers are attracted and turned into ruthless beings.

This is the story of those teenagers.

Morton Rhue, May 2008

4 **ruthless:** rücksichtslos

Editorial note

During my research for "Ghetto Kidz" I spoke with ghetto residents, even gang members, in and around New York City. In addition I read many books and articles on the subject. The following is a selection of them:

Malcolm W. Klein: The American Street Gang: Its Nature, Prevalence and Control, Oxford University Press 1995.

Alex Kotlowitz: There Are No Children Here, Anchor Books 1991.

Jonathan Kozol: The Shame of the Nation: The Restoration of Apartheid Schooling in America, Crown 2005.

Adrian Nicole LeBlanc: Random Family: Love, Drugs, Trouble, and Coming of Age in the Bronx, Scribner 2003.

I recommend the following three articles:

"An Economic Analysis of a Drug-Selling Gang's Finances" by Steven D. Levitt and Sudhir Alladi Venkatesh, in: The Quarterly Journal of Economics.

"A Poverty of the Mind" by Orlando Patterson, in: The New York Times.

"Preventing Adolescent Gang Involvement" by Finn-Aage Esbensen, in: The Juvenile Justice Bulletin.

There is a vast amount of information on gangs on the internet. I'd like to mention two websites that struck me as especially detailed and informative.

The Street Gangs Resource Center (www.streetgangs.com)

The Office of Juvenile Justice and Delinquency Prevention (www.ojjdp.ncjrs.org)